Meetings with Meaning

A Guide to Strategic Collaboration

By Greta Rask

To my father and mother.
You are true professionals,
always voicing what you
believe in.

You inspire me.

TITLE: MEETINGS WITH MEANING

- A GUIDE TO STRATEGIC COLLABORATION

PUBLISHER: GRETA RASK

THE AUTHOR MAY BE CONTACTED AT:

GRETA@RASKUTVECKLING.SE

COVER DESIGN AND INTERIOR DESIGN: NINA PRINGLE

ILLUSTRATIONS: NINA PRINGLE

WWW.NINAPRINGLE.COM

PRODUCED BY VULKAN.SE

PRINTED IN RIGA

ISBN: 978-91-637-5254-4

Contents

The structure of this book

This book consists of three parts that together provide you with knowledge and ideas for how to plan, implement and follow up "meetings with meaning". All theories and models are linked to real life examples. Each chapter concludes with what I call "think slow", aiming to guide you in how you can connect the described models and approaches to your meetings and change projects.

The book begins with:

Part One - About Meaningful Involvement and Change

Part One is largely connected to the belief that we, as human beings, are naturally geared for meaning and connection with others, and we want to be involved in matters that concern us. I explore the importance of mindful and transparent involvement, as well as how we can treasure and connect with people's engagement in the task at hand. I will also describe how meaningful involvement can be used during the life of a change process.

Part Two takes into account that today's reality is rich and complex, both in terms of organizational life and the challenges and opportunities we face. I describe how we can plan and design meetings where diverse people can collaborate fruitfully around a shared concern, and make the most of their differences.

In Part Three I explore the art of mindful facilitation, which is necessary since our genuine engagement awakens our power and our vulnerability. I also discuss the importance of thoughtful follow-up and feedback.

Preface by Jenny Öhman Persson

Doctor of Human Computer Interaction, experienced in research and practice with organizational development and change in a variety of settings.

Dear reader,

Meetings are powerful and thus important to take seriously. Whether they are good or bad, meetings affect us. They can be energizing and inspiring, as well as draining, and even devastating. To develop efficient and effective organizations, the objective, scope and direction have to be clear, and the cultural setting needs to encourage meaningful involvement. This book is about how to create preconditions for successful development and how to deal with the challenges we meet when collaborating in working life. It takes into consideration the need to develop the ability to truly and respectfully involve people, and to do it consciously through meetings with meaning.

I have had the great opportunity to work with Greta in the sub-Saharan African context; in groups with people from many different countries and with different positions, all in the same workshop. With Greta as facilitator, the workshops have always turned out successfully, despite the challenges. In this book, Greta has compiled her in-depth knowledge and skillful ability to design and make meetings meaningful for every participant in such a way that it enhances the professional good. I believe that this book can be useful for everyone in the everyday process of the development of an organization, workshop, meeting or any other professional setting.

Thank you Greta for sharing this!

Jenny Öhman Persson

Introduction

Making a case for Meetings with Meaning

My journey to meetings with meaning began in 1997.

They were stuck. Going in circles around a tricky and hot issue. I was asked to help get them back on track, to provide some structured conversations into their meeting. I still recall the joy I experienced as I saw their body language change, their conversations turn lively and passionate, and their judgments about each other turn into curiosity. That is where my passion for designing and facilitating task focused meetings started.

This experience brought fruitful perspectives to my work with leadership development. For a number of years I had been running leadership programs and witnessed managers struggling to translate what they learned into reality. The conflict resolution skills I was teaching leaders were meaningfully put into practice in the management meetings I facilitated. The personal awareness we wanted leaders to develop came naturally as the climate for conversation was facilitated.

My cultural background largely influences my work with meetings with meaning. I grew up in Sweden, a country known for using a consensus approach. This involves giving those concerned the opportunity to have their say on a matter before reaching a decision that everyone can stand behind. With its spirit of cooperation and trust in the value of different views, it is in many ways a constructive approach.

Yet, I believe it is time to re-evaluate and "upgrade" consensus as a strategy for business development since it can make involvement processes blurry and decision-making unclear, and at times too slow.

Working with individuals' growth, as a coach and therapeutic counselor, also impacts my approach to involvement processes. I know how vulnerable and powerful we become when we get in touch with our passion and sense of meaning.

Finally, the main source of inspiration for how I relate to working and living is Gestalt, as philosophy, theory and methodology. Yet, understanding the models and approaches described in this book doesn't require any prior knowledge of Gestalt. If you are curious and want to know more, there are some reading suggestions at the end of this book and you are welcome to visit my website: www.raskutveckling.com.

> *"Gestalt is an applied philosophy for living.*
> *It is about health, vibrancy, good form and passion."*
>
> Sally Denham-Vaughan[1]

As human beings, we search for meaning and we want to be involved in matters that concern us. We want to voice our opinions and we want to be listened to. Creating something meaningful with others brings us joy. Being part of an organization gives us the opportunity to do just that. In meetings with meaning we use the forces present in all change constructively. We turn resistance into assistance, which becomes possible when we are co-creators of the change. Meetings with meaning can contain the anxiety that is a natural and fruitful part of all high stake challenges, and together we make sustainable change possible.

Increased complexity in many dimensions asks for new ways of meeting. For one, our organizational landscape is becoming increasingly labyrinthine. The era of clear power centers and easily described decision and information structures is over. The traditional line organization still exists, and lives alongside matrix, process, project and network organizations. Teams are required to come together and be efficient quickly. We may work in a number of teams at the same time, some of which can be virtual. This web of relationships requires us to meet and create across traditional boundaries; be they organizational, hierarchical or related to competence, experience, age, geography or culture. And we may need to connect and work with people we barely know, or might never meet in real life.

Also, many of the challenges and tasks that today's organizations are responsible for are complex and urgent. Whether it is complying with new standards on a global market, reducing pesticides and water consumption in the production of cotton, including marginalized groups in our societies, or strengthening our competitive advantage as new strong players enter our markets. A consequence of the urgency and the speed of change is that we don't always have time to do thorough, fact-based analyses. If we did, by the time the analysis is on the table reality has changed. Bringing a diverse group of people together, focusing on a task of mutual concern is often the best we can do, and meetings with meaning can produce surprisingly high quality thinking and ideas.

I meet managers, project leaders and change agents who have a genuine need and wish to involve diverse people in development work, but lack the knowledge and approaches for how to go about it. Involvement can easily end up in "as-if" processes. Meetings that lead nowhere, or participants who feel disappointed that their ideas have not been taken into consideration, or believing that they haven't. People can feel manipulated and participatory processes can lead to change-fatigue. Sadly, meetings can also become an arena for organizational politics and draining power struggles. The meaning and joy I experience in my work with meetings with meaning tells me that it doesn't need to be like this. I witness daily people's innate engagement turn into fuel for the change-fire, and emotional storms within and between people become energy that leads us forward.

This book is inspired by three fundamental beliefs:

1. As human beings, we are naturally geared for meaning and connection with others, and we want to be involved in matters that concern us.

2. Today's organizational landscape is rich and complex. Many of the challenges and opportunities we face in our organizations are also complex, urgent, and frequently controversial. To deal with them in a responsible and meaningful way we need to involve people with diverse backgrounds, in all respects. And we need to support people to connect and create together.

3. Our genuine engagement awakens our power and our vulnerability, and therefore needs to be handled mindfully.

My passion for contributing to meetings with meaning started to grow some sixteen years ago. Hundreds of meetings later, I wish to share my experience of how to treasure and care for people's knowledge, experience and genuine engagement in change and development work in organizations.

As my reader, I believe you belong to one or several of the following groups:

- **A manager at any level.** In this book I refer to you as the task or meeting owner. Most probably you lead and facilitate many meetings yourself – regular management or team meetings, as well as a variety of task-focused workshops. You are the person responsible for the task that is the reason for the meeting, as well as the quality of the output of the meeting. You might face the challenge of leading meetings that require your active participation, and at the same time you have a stake in the outcome. That is, you are never neutral to the task at hand. For these reasons and others you might at times contract a professional facilitator, internally or externally, to help you plan, design and facilitate challenging meetings.

- **A project leader or change agent** with a similar agenda as a manager, but with slightly different challenges.

- **An internal or external process consultant,** who supports leaders in planning, designing and facilitating high stake meetings.

- Or maybe you are just **interested in how we can make our organizations a fertile ground for growth – of business, people and our environment.**

My hope is that this book will give you inspiration, courage and guidance. Whoever you are, I invite you to dive into the exciting world of meetings with meaning. I wish you a meaningful read, and hope to hear from you, as I am curious to see if these ideas make sense to you and your organization.

Greta Rask

Part One

About Meaningful Involvement and Change

Inclusion

"By bringing new voices together, new conversations can happen, new perspectives can emerge, new passions can be aroused and new possibilities for the future can arise."

Jack Martin Leith[2]

Working with a diverse group of people on a matter of common concern is challenging and exciting. Still, we seem to create obstacles for involving others, even when we clearly see a need for it. This part of the book will explore some of the most common doubts I encounter, as well as give a framework for thinking around transparent involvement and how we can link it to people's engagement in the task at hand. You will also get an idea of how to connect meaningful involvement to leading change. With a variety of examples I hope to inspire you to see how you can maximize the effect of your change initiatives by using meaningful involvement during the life of a change process.

1.1. I want to involve people, BUT... - Levels of Involvement

"I want my co-workers to feel involved... BUT I fear I will lose control..."

"I want to involve my team in the business development work... BUT top management has already decided so there is no room to influence the decisions...."

"I really need input from a number of different stakeholders in order to make the right decision… BUT, there is too much controversy and tension around this issue. Fruitful discussions are impossible…"

"I want to involve my managers in the change process… BUT there are still so many undecided variables, things I can't speak openly about…"

"I want to involve people in this change, BUT there is no time for that, we need to implement YESTERDAY…"

"I would like to involve people… BUT they don't seem to care the way I do…"

"I want to invite 20 people from different parts of the organization… BUT how can you get any meaningful work done with such a large group…?"

"I would really like to involve my co-workers… BUT not Jill and Rob, they are so resistant to the change…"

"I know you're supposed to involve people to get their buy-in… BUT to be honest, I believe I have the best solutions myself…"

"I used to believe in involvement, BUT I have grown sick and tired of it, and so has the rest of our organization. It has proven to be a waste of time. What we need is clarity and action…"

These are some of the most common doubts that I meet in managers, project leaders and change agents. In this and the following chapters, I will shed light on some of these BUTS.

Mindful involvement

Involving or manipulating

Our culture influences the way we see involvement. In a predominantly hierarchical culture it is widely accepted that managers choose a low level of involvement. The Swedish culture is, relative to many other cultures, less focused on hierarchy and known for its appreciation of a consensual leadership style. Unfortunately, consensus (from latin consentio – *feel together*) has become more or less synonymous with reaching unanimous agreements. When unanimity is the goal we may strive to make people "feel involved", which can be both time-consuming and deceiving, as the experience of being manipulated lurks around the corner. While there are times when unanimity (latin uno animus - *with one spirit*) is well worth striving for, there are many more situations where we need people to collaborate on strategic issues without needing them to agree, nor to make decisions. By clarifying to what extent people can contribute and influence we can make the most of the consensus approach, and at the same time avoid the trap of unwarily taking people hostage in change initiatives. Because when we do, it generally gives them two options, either to openly show their frustration or, which in many organizational cultures is more likely, to pretend they are on-board.

Transparent involvement

Describing different "levels of involvement" has proven immensely helpful in a variety of cultural contexts: in Asia, Africa, the US and South and North Europe. It challenges us to choose a suitable level of involvement depending on the complexity and context of the task. Consequently, we can be clear and transparent to ourselves as task-owners and facilitators, as well as to those we involve. Clarity on the room to maneuver helps us honor people's engagement, as well as our own integrity and sense of responsibility for the challenges we face.

Levels of involvement

Giving orders or informing

Giving orders or telling people how to do things is undoubtedly a low level of involvement. The analysis is made and so is the decision on what to do and how to do it, but we need to inform those concerned in a clear and pedagogical way to ensure that the decisions lead to action. When the decision is simple, non-controversial and the implementation is pretty straightforward, this is probably the correct level of involvement to opt for. Nonetheless, it is not uncommon to see this level of involvement being used when in fact, both the solutions decided upon as well as the implementation process would have benefited from a higher level of involvement.

Creating shared meaning

A higher level of involvement could be described as creating shared meaning of a decision. A more common way of describing this level of involvement is anchoring, or implementing a decision. Somehow, these terms seem to have lost their original meaning as they are often used to state that the concerned parties have been informed, but don't always indicate that people understand and act in accordance with the decision.

Decisions that are controversial or need a change in attitude, knowledge or motivation in order to be fully implemented require much more than information. Those concerned need time to digest the implications of the decision. In what way is it fruitful for our business? Why this solution? What other options have been considered? How will I be affected? How will it affect our team? How do we turn the decision into action? What do we need from each other and from management for a successful implementation? How is this decision connected to the bigger picture?

Creating shared meaning – an example

"Every year, after getting a go-ahead from our board on the business plan, we have a kick-off with everyone in the organization, all in all about 90. The normal procedure is that we spend the first day presenting the business plan, enjoy a nice dinner and some fun in the evening. Day two, we invite some interesting speakers to share something of value to our business. The days are appreciated and help us create a sense of team spirit for the coming year. This year, we want to do something different, something that leads to more concrete results in the business, and some more sustainable shifts in our people. It's a big investment, two days, overnight..."

They chose to focus on three key aspects of their business plan, digging deeply into their meaning for the business and for the people. A reflection from the meeting owner (the top manager) beautifully summarized the difference they experienced:
"Normally I feel a sense of relief after these two days, a deep sigh, telling me that finally we're done! We've worked so intensely with the business plan, presented it to the board, received their OK and then presented it to our co-workers... But now I realize that it's actually NOW that the real work begins! And that I am not alone doing it!"

Consulting or asking for input
Maybe you as a manager, project leader or change agent have an idea about something you want to do. Maybe even a great idea, and yet you realize that there are other perspectives worth taking into account before moving ahead. You may also have no idea. You see that there is a challenge but you don't have enough information or understanding to decide on how to handle it.

You may choose the level of involvement I call consulting, or asking for input. Considering your task, you invite a group of people with an exciting and relevant mix of knowledge and experience and ask them to elaborate on, and challenge your idea. Or you might ask them to develop the background against which you can decide on the next steps. You are transparent with your belief that you, after the meeting, will be wiser and thereby able to make a strong decision, or that you will know how to proceed with the issue. And you commit to giving feedback to the group on your conclusions and next steps.

Consulting or asking for input – an example

"We urgently need a strategy for our internal and external communication. But as globally responsible, I don't know enough to make a comprehensive and sharp strategy – and I'm aware that the opinions on this topic are strong and diverse in our organization. I need help from those who have a stake in this, as well as from people with knowledge regarding regulations and other boundaries, and from people with strong opinions on the matter – those who can become show-stoppers if they are not on board."

This involvement process was urgent. For years, the organization had struggled with how to communicate on matters related to their serious work with improving environmental as well as social conditions for people involved in their production line. In global organizations, where different parts contribute different things, it is often a challenge to get people aligned on clear messages. The person responsible for communicating globally on this topic needed input from a diverse group of people to be able to put together a communication strategy. This draft strategy was to be presented to the Global management team a few months later.

Being the task owner, she decided to organize a one-day meeting with people from sales, production, communication and external cooperation partners. Not only did she get valuable input to the strategy, the participants also got new insights regarding the complexity of this task, and they mobilized an interest in, and need for the upcoming communication strategy.

Creating a basis for decision

When management wants and/or needs to remain in control of a decision and yet there is significant room to influence, you can invite people to create a basis for decision. This is often experienced as highly engaging. Just remember to have a clear step-by-step plan on how, when and by whom the final decision will be made, as well as how and when the involved parties will receive feedback.

The task-owner decides what the basis for decision should contain and clarifies any relevant boundaries.

Creating a basis for decision – an example

"We are working with our new direction, trying to find out where to position our business in the competitive landscape in five years, as well as figuring out how to get there. We have a clear process that we follow, and a project group is in place for carrying out the analysis and other work that needs to be done. But we realize that we need to have the whole pipeline in the room to pin down the really strong drivers of change."

A two-day meeting was organized with invitees involved in the entire production and sales process. That is, co-workers from different organizational entities, from different parts of the world as well as external stakeholders.

The goal of the meeting was to define a draft to a desired position for this business five years ahead, as well as 3-5 change drivers that would really move the business in the desired direction.

The person responsible for the business was the owner of the meeting. People from the "New direction project group" were present and responsible for carrying the meeting's result forward, as well as for providing feedback to the meeting participants.

Collaborating around a shared challenge or opportunity

In all organizations there are challenges that parts of the organization cannot handle without the involvement of other parts. And there are many challenges that one organization cannot manage without collaborating with other organizations. Sadly, by avoiding to take shared responsibility we can sometimes see how unresolved issues go on for years. We see blame games turning into a way of living. We also see plenty of poor decisions made by knowledgeable people, but based on a limited view of a matter. Each part seems to have done their job, and still the end result is far from satisfactory. In these situations inviting people to 'collaborate around a shared challenge' may be the right level of involvement to opt for. We get the concerned parties together and help them explore the bigger picture and how they, together, can handle their shared challenges in order to deliver successfully to customers, society or other stakeholders. With today's rich complexity in so many dimensions, there is an increasing need for these kinds of meetings.

Collaborating in new constellations often creates unexpected outcomes. For example, to combat vandalism and other petty crime, a community could gather local business owners, police, social workers, youth, parents and city planners. Through creatively using their different perspectives they may end up not only decreasing crime, but also increasing business good-will, as well as creating a stronger network around young people who are struggling.

These types of meetings may involve delegating decision power to the meeting.

Collaborating around a shared challenge – an example

"We are not keeping our promise to our customers. We don't manage to deliver our products on time. The problem is not new, for years

we've had difficulties synchronizing our product development process with production capacity and logistics. We've tried blaming it on poor business systems, as that seems reasonably easy to fix but we've come to the uncomfortable conclusion that it's also people related. Maybe it's the physical distance between us, or a lack of understanding and respect for our different realities and needs... or our cultural differences... Anyhow, it's time we meet and sort out whatever needs to be sorted out to get this business back on track."

The managers who were responsible for the two most affected parts of the organization invited a group of leaders and key people from their respective team to a four-day meeting. Together they explored several crucial aspects of their collaboration. They ended up making sustainable agreements that would ensure delivery on the promise they had made to their customers.

Co-creating – when decision-making is delegated to the meeting
To clearly delegate the power to make decisions to a meeting is still relatively rare, but on the increase. There are strong forces for this, such as the speed of change and the complexities of our tasks, in combination with people's call for being involved. Searching for the perfect analysis or the optimal decision takes too long, and we rarely have time for the inevitable delay that top-down change involves.

We can ensure a "good-enough" quality in analyses and decisions by involving enough diversity in knowledge, experience and motivation. We can also expect a higher level of engagement as well as a considerably swifter implementation by making sure that those who will live the decisions have co-created the analysis, formulated the challenges and decided on the solutions. My understanding of the force against delegating decision-making to a meeting is that it goes against most of our notion of hierarchy and distribution of power. Here are a few examples of when co-creating can be beneficial.

Co-creating – some examples

When many stakeholders need to agree for anything to happen, such as cleaning up the Baltic Sea or putting an end to vandalism in schools, co-creating is an appropriate level of involvement. Creating a CSR strategy (Corporate Social Responsibility) in a global enterprise is another good example. It is an area that poses new challenges by the minute and would simply take too long to create in a more traditional way - asking for input, creating drafts, and sending out for comments. Given its complexity, a high level of involvement increases the likelihood that the strategy will do its job, i.e. affect the way we go about doing our business.

A steering group meeting can be held at this level of involvement, depending on the distribution of power in the project organization. Sometimes the decision power stays with the assignor, and the steering group is advisory. I see a shift towards delegating the power to decide to steering groups, and there are good reasons for that. Many projects deal with high stake, urgent matters that cut across the line organization. So we are handling high complexity in two dimensions, task and process. A lot of time and energy is normally put into creating a project organization that will ensure that all important aspects are covered. However, having all aspects covered on an organization chart doesn't ensure anything, while a meaningful steering-group meeting can. I have seen how giving decision-power to a steering group has contributed to better planning of their meetings. As tension is a normal and fruitful ingredient in steering group meetings, they require a purposeful design and competent facilitation.

"For the really high stake projects that we run in our business I as CEO tend to be the formal assignor. It goes without saying that it's impossible for me to stay on top of all these complex and urgent projects, I rely completely on the wisdom of my steering groups.

A while back I admitted to myself that they weren't as wise as I thought... and that I played a large part in their shortcomings, our shortcomings I should say. As tensions rose, it could be when the issues on the table shuffled power, or when there was a lot of ambiguity around the challenge at hand, we could end up spending a whole meeting on the first point on the agenda, leaving the remaining five to be dealt with outside the meeting. And somehow, when things got really heated, they all looked at me. This was clearly a waste of time of already busy people as well as detrimental for the quality of our projects and, not to forget, demotivating for our project leaders and their teams.

We've made several changes. The first one seemed tough, but proved to be relatively easy. We significantly decreased the number of people in our steering groups. When seeing myself in the mirror I realized that I, and others, often designed the groups based on some vague idea of involvement, that he or she had to be there in order to feel involved in the issue. Or, which was even tougher to admit, that I assigned people as steering group members out of fear. If I didn't allow him or her into the living room so to speak, she/he could obstruct the whole idea after decisions were taken. Making this change has made me more courageous and transparent, which I think the whole company will benefit from. And I think I've finally understood the difference between compliance and commitment. I used to settle with compliance, but I've learned that it's an ocean of difference in the quality of people's work when they are truly committed.

Other changes we've made are clear delegation of decision-power to the steering group meetings, which has made us all responsible and accountable for the quality of our work and our decisions. We have also decided to have a professional facilitator present in all high stake steering group meetings. That has allowed me to fully participate in the meeting. The tension is still there, but now we use it for the benefit of the task and our people. I believe that we now, by making good use of our differences in the meeting room, can meet the organization with much more clarity and determination when implementing our decisions."

Think of a meeting you attended recently. To what level of involvement were you invited? Was it made clear to you or are you guessing? How did that clarity or lack of clarity affect your level of engagement in the meeting? What would have made a difference for you?

If you are planning a meeting in the near future, to what level of involvement do you want to invite your meeting participants? Do you want to:

- *Give orders or inform?*
- *Create shared meaning?*
- *Consult or ask for input?*
- *Create a basis for decision?*
- *Collaborate around a shared challenge?*
- *Co-create – where decision-making is clearly delegated to the meeting?*

If your meeting involves several tasks, would it make sense to choose different levels of involvement for the different tasks?

If you are clear in your mind about what level you are inviting to, what difference do you think it will make for the energy and participation in the meeting? What difference will it make for the outcome of the meeting? And what difference will it make after the meeting?

Imagine…
If most people attending meetings in your workplace knew to what level of involvement they were invited, what would happen…

1.2. Do they really want to be involved? - Levels of Engagement

As human beings we want to be involved in matters that concern us, and naturally our level of engagement differs depending on our relationship to the task. My understanding of how an issue affects my life and work will have an impact on my level of engagement. Maybe I'm generally unimpressed by budgets and numbers, but when I see how the activities I'm engaged in may be affected by an increase or decrease in margins, I might want to participate in a change process for improved margin revenue.

It can also be worthwhile to challenge how my own perception of the meaning of a task can influence my judgment of whether others could be engaged. In other words, what is boring to me might be of great interest to others who are closer to the task and vice versa.

Indifference

Being indifferent is non-existent engagement. It is close to apathy. People are rarely indifferent in relation to change or development at work that affects them. And yet I sometimes hear: *"I would like to involve my team but they don't seem to care."* A lack of engagement can be the result of a culture where people are not being listened to, where creativity is regarded as a job for a few creative specialists, where good ideas are neither asked for nor appreciated or where one is punished for making mistakes.

It can also be the result of too many "as-if-processes", meaning that too many times people have been invited to contribute at a high level of involvement, or so they were led to believe, but in reality the decision had already been made. Or, it might be that we have a history of failing in the feedback process.

Low engagement can also be the result of a culture where change initiatives are often taken but rarely followed through. Of course that has an impact on people's trust, *"there is no point contributing, nothing will happen anyway..."*

If you recognize yourself in any of the above, it is just about making your mind up. When you are serious about the change and your intent to involve, the people you invite will feel that and their trust in you as well as their engagement will grow, step by step. But in case you are thinking of involving someone who honestly doesn't care, then don't.

Curiosity

Being curious is a certain level of engagement, not much, but a little. It can be enough to be invited to a 'meaning-making' process, but doesn't suffice when we want people to create a strong basis for decision or to co-create. However, curiosity can open the emotional door to increased engagement. There are many meetings where I've witnessed people move from tepid curiosity to burning engagement.

A wish to learn

To come to an involvement process with the intention of learning something is a slightly higher level of engagement than curiosity, but not enough when invited to a high level of involvement. Having said that, the openness that a wish to learn brings to an involvement process is great for the dynamics of any group.

A wish to contribute

Harrison Owen, the founder of Open Space Technology[3], has an elegant way of putting it, *"If you are not here to learn or to contribute, use your feet."* As I understand it, it is just a way of stating the obvious. If the participants don't want to learn anything, nor contribute to the work, there will be no results and it is perfectly all right to leave the room. Nevertheless, openly admitting that you don't want to learn or contribute can be risky in some organizations. When that is the case, it is safer to ensure people's engagement as much as we can before the meeting.

A wish to take co-responsibility

The highest level of engagement can be described as a wish to take co-responsibility. When you choose the highest level of involvement, to co-create and delegate decision-making, inviting people that want to take co-responsibility is a precondition. Not only to achieve the best possible decisions, but also to ensure engagement in the implementation phase.

Resistance – a form of engagement

So where is resistance on the scale of engagement? It is easy to see resistance as a lack of engagement. But upon closer observation it is most often an expression of strong engagement. We need to remind ourselves that resistance is a law of nature. There is resistance in all change processes. When the resistance is invited into the change process it creates the friction needed to move forward. Resistance becomes assistance. When the resistance is blocked out, it easily turns destructive *and* we miss out on the refinement of ideas that resistance brings to any process. There's more on the forces present in change in Part One, chapter 4, page 41.

How they are connected – Levels of involvement and levels of engagement

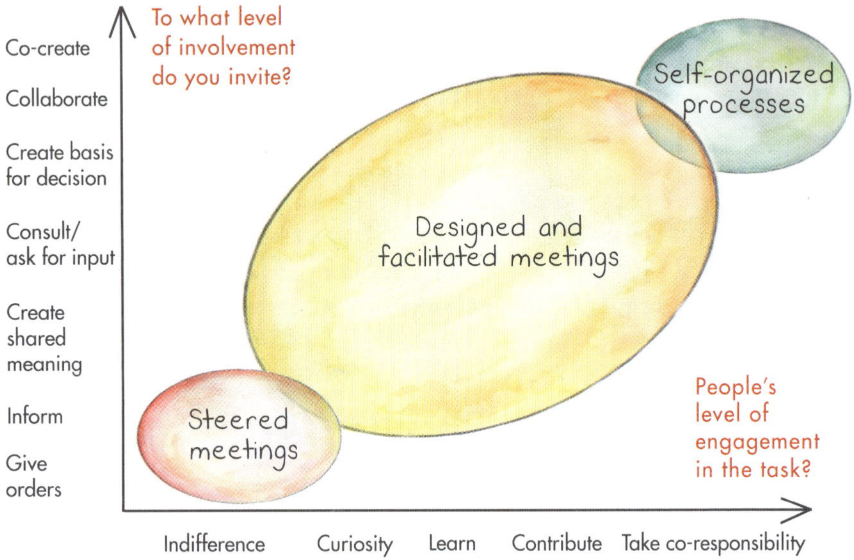

The model above[4] gives an overview of how levels of involvement and levels of engagement interact, as well as how they are connected to different types of meetings. People's level of engagement needs to be reasonably correlated to the level of involvement we invite them to. If highly engaged people are invited to a low level of involvement their motivation will drop and they will lose trust in their leaders. Inviting people who are not engaged to a high level of involvement is equally pointless.

Steered meetings do not require much knowledge about human dynamics and is therefore not within the scope of this book. I don't touch much on self-organized processes, as I don't experience them to be the main focus for today's organizations. This book is about what I call designed and facilitated meetings, which I believe is a step towards more self-organizing processes.

Think of a meeting you attended recently. How engaged were you in the task at hand? Were you:

- *Indifferent?*
- *Curious?*
- *Interested in learning?*
- *Willing to contribute?*
- *Willing to take co-responsibility?*

What do you think contributed to your level of engagement in the meeting? What could have increased your engagement? Did your level of engagement grow or decrease during the course of the meeting? If so, why?

If you are planning a meeting in the near future, what level of engagement among the participants is necessary for achieving the results you desire?

What is within your power to do before the meeting, to ensure that the participants are sufficiently engaged in the task by the time the meeting will take place?

Imagine…
If most people attending meetings in your workplace were engaged in the task of the meeting, if participants came to meetings with a willingness to learn, contribute and even take co-responsibility, what would happen…

1.3. Choosing Level of Involvement

Guiding questions for choosing level of involvement

There are five aspects to consider when determining the level of involvement we should invite people to: the complexity of the task, the implementation time-span, the room to influence decisions, our courage to deal with anxiety and our belief about people's ability to contribute.

1. The complexity of the task
A complex task needs to be looked upon from many different angles in order to find a sustainable way forward. We probably need highly engaged people who are willing to contribute with their knowledge, wisdom and passion. They will most likely expect to be involved to a relatively high level in order to contribute to the extent that you need. This informs you to move upwards in the levels of involvement.

2. The implementation time-span
If you need a swift implementation of a decision, it is wise to invite to a rather high level of involvement. If those affected by the decisions are involved in the analysis and decision-making, their sense of meaning and understanding for the totality increases. Subsequently, their engagement and energy in the implementation phase is likely to be greater.

3. The room to influence decisions
Sometimes the room to influence decisions is less than you wish. This is one of the dilemmas of every manager and it is important not to close our eyes to these limitations. There are times when it is possible to stretch the boundaries. And when it is not, or if you as the responsible manager or project leader choose not to fight for more freedom, you need to take a reality check before choosing level of involvement.

4. Our courage to deal with anxiety
In high stake meetings anxiety is a natural and fruitful ingredient, so are differences of opinion and the possibility of conflict. Many people find these kinds of tensions uncomfortable and are unsure of their capacity to handle it.

When we are genuinely engaged in collaboration with others we are vulnerable. Ambivalence, insecurity and differences of opinion are necessary ingredients in any involvement process that is about real change or development. It only takes subtle signals from a task-owner for an individual or a group to suppress doubts, insecurities or differences. And when that happens, the process dies. As task-owners we have our own opinions and might take sides prematurely in the process, which can silence the differences that we need and ask for. It is important to be aware of these dilemmas, and to take our concerns seriously. If we come to the conclusion that we won't be able to handle the process in a constructive way, we have two choices; either we can ask an experienced facilitator – someone we feel safe with – for help, or we refrain from group involvement processes.

5. Our beliefs about people's capacity to contribute
Do I believe that people have the capacity to contribute to the refinement of an idea, analyze a tricky situation, or creatively handle a challenge or cease opportunities? If not, let's not involve them.

How can we influence people's engagement?
The communication around any change or development initiative is fundamental for engagement. If the communication strategy is well thought through, we will influence people's engagement prior to any involvement meeting.

During a meeting with meaning there are predominantly three factors that affect the engagement:

1. Super clarity on the task – what are they here to achieve and what are the relevant boundaries? See Part Two, chapter 2, page 73.

2. The design of the meeting, see Part Two, chapter 4, page 83.

3. The facilitation of the meeting, see Part Three, chapter 1, page 114.

Think of a meeting you attended recently. What do you believe influenced the task-owner/meeting owner's choice of level of involvement?

- *The complexity of the task?*
- *The implementation time-span?*
- *The room to influence decisions?*
- *The meeting owner's courage to deal with anxiety?*
- *His or her belief about people's ability to contribute?*

If you are planning a meeting in the near future, which of these five aspects are relevant for you to consider in your planning process?

Imagine…
If most meeting owners in your workplace made an honest evaluation while planning meetings, considering the five aspects mentioned above, how would that effect your meetings…

1.4. About Change and Involvement

Mindful involvement is key to successful change. When we understand and appreciate the dynamics present in all change, its cyclical nature and its sources of resistance, we run a better chance of involving the right people, to the right level, at the right time.

"We seem to be in for a bumpy road... let's all buckle up and enjoy the ride".

Tom Stratton[5]

The dynamics of change

There are some characteristics of change that, if we take them to heart, can help us understand and make good use of the dynamics present in all change processes.

The force for change – and the force for keeping what is
In all change there is a force for change, and a force for keeping what is. That is how systems work. Sadly, we have a tendency to personalize these forces as in *"John is always a driver of change, and Darryl is so resistant"*. There is also a risk of seeing the force

for change as a source of energy and the force for resistance as a lack of energy, kind of like a concrete wall that is blocking change initiatives. In fact there is energy in both forces, and there is engagement in both forces.

Force creates counterforce

Force creates counterforce. So when we push people into changing, they will push back. *"It's not that I don't like change, I just don't like being changed"*. In organizational life, our pushing can be rather sophisticated. We can try our best to convince others that our ideas are great, closing our ears and eyes to people's doubts. Or we might, sometimes unwittingly, manipulatively coerce others into doing what we want them to do. When we are very attached to our ideas, subtle protesting such as a frown, a glance, a *yes, but…* can easily pass us by.

Often, there is a delay in the "pushing back" and it can come in forms that are even difficult to connect to my pushing. When people say YES and smile, and yet you see no action, you know some retaliation is happening. Without supporting people in making sense of change initiatives, the most we can ever hope for is compliance. When we are looking for commitment, we need a different approach.

Seeing and appreciating the forces

To understand the forces present in change, we can reflect on societal change. As democratic movements become increasingly powerful we see a counterforce growing, sometimes even in fundamentalist movements. And we know that strengthening women in developing countries has the greatest impact when the men in the community are involved.

We can also increase our understanding of these forces by taking a closer look at ourselves. Even when change is self-imposed, the forces are present. I might be highly motivated to adopt a healthier life-style, and still there is a force in me for keeping what is, whether it is cozy evenings in front of the TV or sleeping in rather than rising at 5.30 to go to the gym. It may be clear to me that I would be a more successful leader if I kept my hands off once I have delegated a task, and I can be strongly committed to changing that behavior. Still, at closer look, I discover a competing commitment to perfection. It then makes sense that I resist the change I long for. When I don't acknowledge, and even honor my own resistance, the change is often short-lived.

As leaders of change in organizations we need to be in contact with our own resistance. We may be convinced that moving manufacturing from Poland to China is the right thing to do, and yet there are aspects of the change that evoke resistance in us. When we don't make peace with our own resistance we run the risk of unwarily projecting our resistance onto others, and unproductive knee-jerk reactions is a likely response when faced with resistance – especially when it is our own.

Resistance as assistance

With this understanding we invite the resistance into conversations about the change. Resistance is assistance when actively involved in the change process. Resistance creates the friction we need to move forward in a constructive way. Many companies are concerned with not being open to change, not being creative, agile and adaptable enough. Yet the challenge of using the resistance is just as urgent. We see loan bubbles pop, over-fishing of impoverished fishing waters, investments in new business systems costing four times the estimated cost. The list goes on. To find sustainable solutions to many of our challenges we need to support differentiation, whereby we can avoid group-think, and we need to cultivate our appreciation for resistance.

The cycle of change

Rick Maurer, a renowned writer, consultant and my teacher at the Gestalt Institute of Cleveland, illustrates the natural and cyclic nature of change in his *"Cycle of Change"*[6]. It supports us to be mindful when working with the forces present in change.

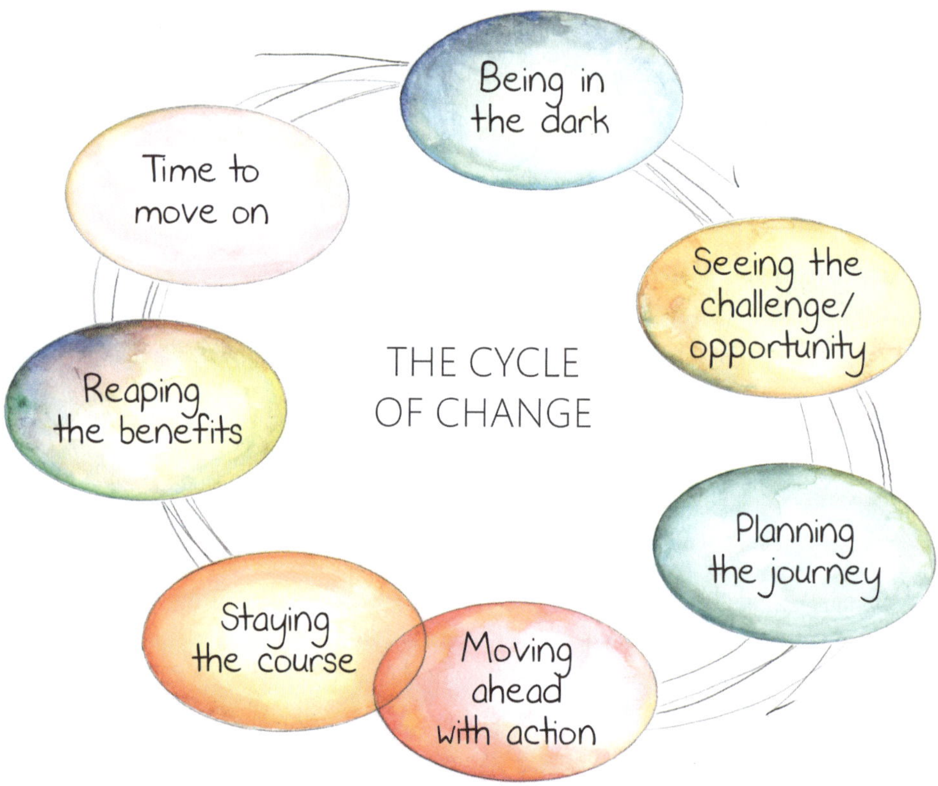

From being in the dark to seeing the challenge/opportunity When we are in the dark we are largely unaware of the need for change. In order for us to well manage the process of going from being in the dark to clearly seeing the challenge or opportunity, we need to gather the signals that call for change into a meaningful whole. This phase of a change process is a great opportunity to make a strong and compelling case for change. By involving broadly we minimize the risk of defining our challenge or opportunity, and thereby the solutions, on a limited view of reality. And simultaneously we can make sure that key stakeholders *"feel the need for change in their guts"*, as Maurer puts it.

In this phase we need to be aware of our natural tendency to paint the current situation in black and the desired future in pink. To make an appealing invitation to join us in change we need to honor the past, acknowledge that today holds its strengths and that our desired tomorrow will inevitably contain its weaknesses and threats.

We also need to keep in mind that what is a compelling case for change for one person in an organization might hold very little meaning for someone else. A management team could and should become alert when new competitors are popping up in far away continents, whereas local sales people might focus their interest on buying behavior among current clients. So what is foreground to some stakeholders could be background to others, and vice versa. It is really about stepping into the shoes of others and seeing the world from their perspective. When we forget to do that, we risk leaving people behind us as well as inviting unnecessary resistance.

Planning the journey

When a critical mass of relevant stakeholders see the challenge we have mobilized the energy we need to step into the next phase, where we create a clear roadmap for the change. It includes clarifying the vision, setting goals and defining milestones along the way; making it possible to monitor the change. Since a good plan is something to hold on to during a bumpy change journey, clear assignments and deadlines are crucial. Make sure your plan includes task- as well as people aspects: does the change require a new set of skills, a different organizational set-up, a change in attitudes and behaviors, a different focus from leaders, alterations in performance follow-ups and reward systems? Building your change plan into your regular business plan supports success, as long as you allocate time for all the hard work that change entails.

When we aim for purposeful involvement also this phase, we create the conditions necessary for commitment rather than mere compliance. We need to make sure to involve those who will live the change; that is the best way to ensure ambitious yet realistic goals and deadlines.

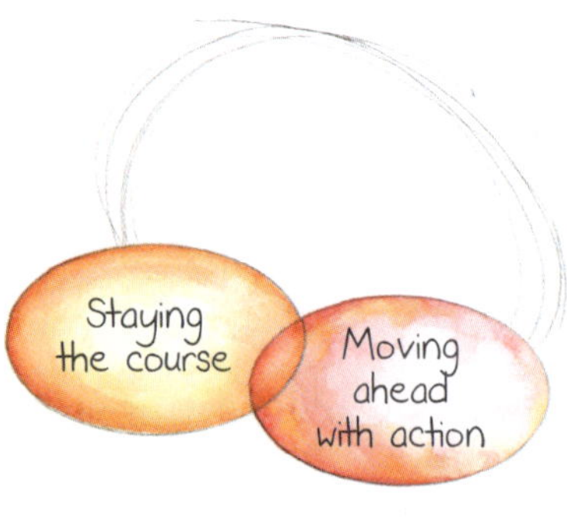

Moving ahead with action and staying the course

We now make the change happen by putting our plan into action. It is about working hard, celebrating successes, learning from failures and above all, staying the course. The risk we face in these phases is thinking that we are done when we have actually just gotten started. If we don't stay with it we easily revert to old habits.

As initiators or owners of the change we must remain engaged and show it. This is the phase of nitty-gritty, which is not for everyone. So in the event we need to move on to other tasks, or if our forte and passion is in the initial phases of change, it is our responsibility to make a clear delegation of the implementation and show that we stand behind that person and/or team.

In this phase many of those concerned by the change are busy doing all the heavy work that implementing change is about, often parallel to conducting their running business. If we don't take care of ourselves and each other, we risk running out of energy. Set time aside for stopping and reflecting – thinking slow – and you will monitor your change process and care for people's energy levels at the same time. The need to say good-bye to whatever we are leaving behind us is likely to emerge, and meaningful ceremonies are supportive at this point. Mindful closures also help us to recharge our batteries.

Reaping the benefits

This is where we reach our destination and enjoy the benefits that the change has brought us. We ensure that we, again and again, act in accordance with the new, i.e. the change is now fully integrated. For this to happen we have made certain that relevant support and follow-up systems are in place, as well as remembered to care for people's need to feel seen and appreciated for their efforts.

We should consider involving people in a symbolic act that emphasizes that we have arrived at our desired destination – or not, if it didn't happen. By creating a common awareness that the change is coming to an end we help people close this cycle and move on to the next phase, getting ready for future needs for change.

Time to move on

Sooner or later we arrive at a point when it is time to move on. Staying alert for the signals of the next needed change is now relevant. This is a place that requires open ears, eyes and heart – and courage, as subtle change signals might be both difficult to spot and uncomfortable to accept.

How involvement can be linked to the cycle of change in the elaboration of a new corporate direction

"Our strategy is coming to an end ('time to move on'). This time around I want to involve a diverse group of people in creating the new strategy. I'd like us to be able to press go once the strategy is finalized, rather than starting the headache-creating process of getting everyone's buy-in... and maybe slowly realizing that we've missed some valuable input along the way. (That is, thoroughly work through the phases 'in the dark' and 'seeing the challenge', before 'planning the journey' and 'moving ahead with action'.)

I want to create a strong and courageous management team. I see us as a sort of hub for whatever change the new strategy will entail. We need to be a group of leaders that our co-workers can trust along a possibly bumpy road. And I want us to actively involve various critical stakeholders during the one year strategizing process, all dependent on the issues we are working with, where we are in the process, and where we see the forces for change and resistance."

So far, their process has involved getting wiser through involving broadly, internal as well as external stakeholders. They have learned about their need for change through sharing stories about the company and its context; now, in the past and for the future. The need for change has emerged with greater and greater clarity. Continuously, as needed, they have invited all leaders and key people in refining ideas and dealing with mishaps along the way. All leaders have been trained in how to lead change and all co-workers have learned about the dynamics of change. Voluntary task forces have developed different aspects of the Direction. Management team members have been available for conversations with teams that express concerns. They have continually updated, as well as received input, from their steering group, their board, main customers and other relevant external stakeholders. They have organized implementation task forces around different aspects of the change. Through continuously keeping an ear to the ground they ensure that they are on track, and that they stay sensitive to the forces for the change, as well as the forces for keeping what is. When called for, they create arenas for meaningful dialogues in cross-functional meetings. In different stages, and with different stakeholders, they have invited people to different levels of involvement. At times it has been important for the management team to keep control of decisions since they in turn present their ideas to a steering group for final decision-making. However, the closer they get to the roll-out phase the more decision power they choose to delegate. It makes sense, especially since this is a company where, historically, people have not been invited to a high level of involvement. There is often a slight learning curve in mobilizing energy for co-creating. Another reason for moving up the involvement ladder is that once the decision on the *what* has been made by the board, the management of the company has more room to influence decisions that they in turn can delegate, when they find it meaningful to do so.

It is tricky to recount a change story with body and soul. It is never linear. It never moves from clarity to clarity. It always involves hanging upside down and there are always surprises and events in people's lives outside of work that affect the journey. In short – it is bumpy. What this story tries to convey is that by understanding the dynamics of change, and combining that understanding with meaningful involvement, we can make the most of every bump. We can prevent a few, and we trust that we will get there – together.

Cherish each cycle – large and small

A change process such as the one described above takes years. Using our own, and other people's energy wisely is literally a question of survival. To support us in doing so, it is helpful to see each phase in the cycle clearly. Using the example above, here is an illustration of how to do that:

- Creating the New Direction – going from 'being in the dark' to 'seeing the challenge'
- Preparing for implementation by defining new roles, clarifying the new organizational set-up, recruitment procedures, etc. – 'planning the journey'
- Putting the new organization and business processes in place, monitoring and learning – this is 'moving ahead with action and staying the course'
- Securing that we've arrived at our destination – 'reaping the benefits'
- Being open for future needs for change – 'time to move on'

Each phase of the change can also be seen as its own cycle of change, and even within each phase there are cycles. Planning and conducting an information meeting for all staff regarding the new organizational set-up is a cycle, defining roles in the new organization is a cycle, and so is each recruitment for the new positions. And every development talk with a co-worker, supporting them in understanding the change and connecting with their own wishes going forward, is a cycle of change. Ending each small and large cycle with a deep breath, celebrating what has gone well, and learning from our mistakes – helps us make closure and recharge our batteries. Real change is exhausting so we need every extra breath we can take.

Running parallel change initiatives

"We are running 50 change projects at the same time!" might be going through your mind. This is a reality for many which makes it challenging to manage change with pride. Many organizations need to better synchronize their change initiatives, as well as prioritize much harder. To avoid unnecessary confusion and possible change-fatigue we need to create arenas where we can explore and make shared meaning of how different change projects are connected and contribute to the same overall goal.

Making sense of parallel change projects

In just two years, a company had gone from being present in one country to operating in four countries, as well as moving their production from Scandinavia to China. Their strategy was to buy companies with a similar profile. This involved merging organizational cultures as well as business systems and leadership. The owners needed the new corporate entity to be up to speed quickly, therefore a number of change projects were launched. A year later there was great confusion and hard-working staff was approaching burn-out. Management had clearly underestimated the need for all key stakeholders to 'see the challenge', as well as the complex picture that all the change programs was presenting. They were losing time and the board was impatient. Pushing harder seemed to increase both the confusion and the resistance, so they needed to come up with a different approach. During a management team meeting the issue was finally brought to the table and discussed with candor. It was an emotional meeting with a constructive outcome. They decided to invite all project leaders for key projects to a meeting with management. A "graphic facilitator" was invited to draw representations of the conclusions of the meeting. They ended up with a beautiful illustration of how all the projects were interlinked and connected to the company's strategy and overall goals. This turned out to be a useful tool for middle-managers to communicate meaningfully with their co-workers. And as the magnitude of the projects became clear to decision-makers they decided to put some of the projects on hold, and skip others all together.

Any real change involves hanging upside down
It is likely that we are struggling with a mental map saying that managers know more and should always be on top of things. This is less and less true due to the complexity and speed of change that is today's reality. Any real strategic change means that everyone involved moves through confusion and not knowing, management included. It also means that for change to happen out there – you need to change. Some leaders believe mistakenly that they already "are the change". So it is worth pointing out that, when aiming for purposeful involvement in strategic processes, top management also needs to be involved – developing their understanding together with their organization. It might seem obvious, yet in the excitement of being invited to contribute people can start to expect independence and hands-off from management, especially if management involvement historically has meant *"manager decides and puts the lid on any ideas outside his or her comfort zone"*.

So it requires a certain sensitivity of leaders to manage this balancing act; to not lose touch with the development of ideas, to contribute when needed, and to keep reminding of any relevant boundaries. Thus, by caring for their own mobilization of energy, leaders are ready to act when the time is right.

Leadership commitment matters
Leadership commitment is key to successful change. Sadly, many studies show that 60-70%[7] of change initiatives don't achieve

what they aim for, and some conclude that lack of leadership commitment is one of the major contributors. Building understanding and commitment in the team that is leading the change, and continuing to nurture that commitment, is an investment that always pays off.

Resistance and involvement

The force for keeping what is, or resistance, becomes assistance when invited into dialogue. When marginalized or avoided it quickly turns destructive and can, on top of disruptions to the change process, cause a lot of unnecessary pain.

Good reasons to shy away from resistance
Good intentions of inviting the resistance into dialogue can in the blink of an eye vanish out the window. Resistance is not always expressed in a straightforward way, people may respond to our wants with arrogance, silence, or a "yes, but…" so it makes sense that our defenses kick in. We can hit back by closing our ears, blocking people out or by silencing others in more or less sophisticated ways.

Another reason to turn our backs on resistance is fearing that we will lose our own energy for the change if we listen to others' doubts. This can happen, and here are some plausible reasons for that which are worth exploring. It could be a consequence of not having acknowledged our own resistance to the change, or we might need to remind ourselves that meeting others with an open mind doesn't mean an empty mind. We don't need to give up on our vision, our opinions, the boundaries and non-negotiables, nor does it mean giving up on having expectations on people, or on holding others accountable.

With all my heart I would like to inspire change leaders to mobilize their courage and patience to meet reality as it is. It is so much easier, it involves so much less pain and it is immensely more productive.

If we don't meet and respect people where they are, how can we expect them to join us in change?

Three sources of resistance
Rick Maurer's thinking on resistance and support helps us to increase our awareness of the forces present in our change process. He defines three sources of resistance that are easy to relate to, and fruitful to work with. And they are relational.

I don't get it

'I don't get it' is predominantly an intellectual, or cognitive source of resistance. It has to do with our understanding of the change. Do I see a need for change? Do I have a clear enough picture of the background against which this change initiative is emerging as relevant? If I don't, it is sensible to resist.

To what extent do different important stakeholders in your change process get it? What do you hear people say or what do you see them do that gives you information about their understanding of the change? Where you work, is it OK to say that you don't understand, or to ask for more information? Once you got it, how is your patience with other people's process of creating meaning of the change? How do you adapt your message to successfully reach different stakeholders?

This source of resistance is of course directly linked to our efforts of making a compelling case for change, phases one and two in the cycle, though it remains relevant all through the change process.

I don't like it

This source of resistance involves our emotions. Do I believe I can handle the change? Will my competence still be valid? Will I lose something I cherish, be it tasks, prestige, my manager, colleagues or my job? It is important to remember that when fear is involved, our amygdala[8] is activated and I might literally not hear what you are saying.

The polarity of this source of resistance is excitement about the opportunities the change will bring. This is a place where we wobble; it can be like an emotional roller coaster. *"I can't wait to get started, learn new things, get new colleagues, take on a greater responsibility, move office…! NO, what was I thinking, I will never be able to make it, I will miss this place, these people…"* When wobbling is permitted, and even welcomed, we give ourselves and others the opportunity to grow truly committed to the change. It is easy to see that this source of resistance needs to be met with sensitivity. If your organizational culture doesn't allow vulnerability, it will be difficult to invite and make the most of this source of resistance.

I don't trust you

The third source of resistance is lack of trust in those who are leading the change. People not trusting us is uncomfortable, and therefore easy to avoid paying attention to and addressing. Do I trust that you, the leader or leaders of the change are capable of leading me/us into the desired future?

It hurts not to be trusted. We need to remember that often, the mistrust is not all about us. People might mistrust what we represent, be it the board, top management, my gender, profession, class or culture. Or it can be experiences from the past that make people mistrust us. Perhaps the organization has a history of not following through with change. Asking ourselves whether people have good reasons to trust me/us is worthwhile. Trusting the leaders of change is so fundamental that if we do discard it, we will probably get nowhere with our change initiative.

You could argue that people get it, feel that they can handle it, and even trust the initiator of the change, and yet resist the change because they disagree with the chosen path. When we can safely voice our disagreements and be heard, it can be possible to go along with the change regardless of our own opinions. We can be inspired by the Bahá'í principle for consultation[9] : *"Implementing decisions wholeheartedly, a commitment to unity, ensures that if a decision or project fails, the problem lies in the idea itself, and not in lack of support from the community or the obstinate actions of opponents."* And of course, there are times when people decide not to go along with a decided change, and when that happens we can support them (or ourselves) in making an aware choice of action.

Processing personal resistance to change

"I understand and agree that we need to improve efficiency and cut our staff by 30%. Yet I'm worried, as I know my position is part of the 30% and I have a family to support and the economy is weak; it will be very difficult to find a new job. I do trust management. This is not the first time they've had to downsize due to fierce competition and they have always done what they need to do in a respectful and caring way. I've seen colleagues leave with their heads high. I know that they need me to give my 100% during the implementation of the change; I hope I will manage to do that."

Spotting and working with resistance
Structuring resistance in this way doesn't imply that it is sequential, nor that we can address the sources one at a time and then sit back and trust that everyone is on board. We need to keep our ears and eyes open all through the cycle of change and engage in conversations about the change whenever and wherever it is needed. To stay alert we can use various lenses, such as our list of key stakeholders, or looking at different levels of the system, or different professional roles. What sources of support and resistance am I spotting?

As leaders in change we need to listen beyond words and actions, since the way we express resistance rarely is straightforward. A nod of acceptance and no action can mean that the person doesn't get it, but for some reason is unable to ask for clarifications. Or when many say that they agree with the change, yet don't stop giving you reasons why it won't work. Maybe they don't trust that you will stick with the change – and with them – to the bitter end. Complaints concerning the change may also involve that people feel uncertain about whether they will be able to cope with the change ('I don't like it'). Keeping this in mind makes us humble in relation to resistance, and we will do a better job at keeping people in the loop.

"If there is no resistance to the changes we are initiating, we should be worried. All real change evokes resistance. We need to embrace the resistance - not fear it, fight it, ignore it or shut it out."

Didas Tumuhairwe[10]

Helping people to get it is too often addressed with a presentation (and in worst cases via an internal network), which rarely does the trick of creating understanding – nor does it build trust. People need to talk, reflect and make sense of things in order to get it. When we meet people face to face and make ourselves available for conversation about the change, we simultaneously address resistance related to trust. Talking from our heart, sharing the background or context of the change, being a bit transparent with our own emotional reactions to the change initiative helps a long way. And then, let people talk. As leaders of the change, we have to prick up our ears and listen. Of course, the more willing we are to involve people, the more able they will be to continually bring up concerns related to the change. Consequently, we are more likely to continually build and address issues of trust as a natural part of the process.

Safeguarding our sensitivity to the emotional aspects of resistance is like oil in the change machinery. Depending on the magnitude of the change and on our personal situation we can experience change as an emotional roller coaster. Going through a change process is at times well described by the Cycle of Crisis and Trauma (originally developed by psychiatrist Johan Cullberg): experiencing shock, denial, anger, sadness/grief, and then moving into acceptance and eventually re-orientation. With this in mind we want to establish a working climate where emotions don't need to be withheld, we create arenas for continuous conversations, as well as appropriate ceremonies that help us let go of the past and thereby be more open to embrace the new.

The three sources of resistance at play

A working group consisting of psychiatric nurses, nurses' assistants and psychiatrists entered the room. They were all new to me and attending this meeting was mandatory. The topic of our conversation for the next one and a half hours was the complexity that working with patients who are suicidal entails, with the purpose of strengthening the team's capacity to work with this particularly challenging group of patients. Their body language communicated that they didn't want to be there. They looked at me with suspicion. One man demonstratively pulled his chair back, giving me a critical look. I noticed how my heart rate increased. As I was very engaged in this project I experienced that the group, with their resistance, somehow stepped on my engagement. I centered myself, decided to go slow, not pushing anyone to do or say anything. My nice circle of chairs, that was supposed to support high quality conversation, was now in disorder. I proposed to the group that we hear a little bit from each one, any expectations or hesitations about being there... I pricked up my ears, appreciating whatever little they expressed, connecting one person's comments to another's, and they started to open up a bit. Their comments and behavior could be linked to all three sources of resistance:
"I don't get why we are spending time on this as we among our patients have very few suicides. We have more urgent matters to discuss, like management cutting the number of staff."
"I don't like being here. Talking about stuff like this in our team is too risky, we don't show our vulnerabilities to one another."
"I don't trust you. Even though I don't know you, I don't trust those who sent you here (i.e. management)."

Although this was not expressed explicitly, it came across loud and clear.

In 90 minutes the resistance had turned into support. They expressed that this was time well spent and that they looked forward to our upcoming sessions, well summarized in *"I think having these kinds of conversations can support us in creating a stronger alliance with people who are questioning if life is worth living. If it just helps us save one life, it's well worth it!"* The energy in their resistance turned into engagement in the process going forward.

"We don't trust management"
Below is an example of a change process where the strongest resistance was related to low trust in management, the leaders of the change.

Upgrading the Company Culture

This company was rapidly going from a secure position on the market to experiencing fierce competition. Financially they were already suffering. They described themselves as very hierarchical, slow to react, great at fixing things that went wrong, but weak at securing work processes in order to prevent mistakes. They wanted to change the culture, making sure that their way of working and relating to one another supported their business reality.

This is how the process was designed:
Step 1. Bringing the whole management team from 'being in the dark' to 'seeing the challenge.'
Since only a few members of the management team experienced (or at least expressed) the need for change, the CEO needed to start with his team. Together they explored the organization's

strengths and weaknesses and a shared picture of the need for change emerged. To get the most possible speed in the change, they discussed different ways of designing the change process. The approach they decided on was predominantly inspired by two factors, one was the urgent need to instill a sense of leadership and proactivity among all co-workers. The other inspiration was their own experience of moving from 'being in the dark' to 'seeing the challenge' during a one day focused meeting.

Step 2. Getting the whole system in the room – 'Making a compelling case for change'

They decided to organize a two-day meeting with 30 people using a whole-system-in-the-room approach, meaning that people from all functions and all hierarchical levels were invited. This alone was revolutionary since people rarely or never met across these boundaries, neither were co-workers ever invited to discuss strategic issues. This group of 30 analyzed the company's history, creating a shared understanding and respect for today's culture. They looked at the present situation from different perspectives: competition, owners, business strategy, financial situation, co-workers expectations, etc. (Again, making a compelling case for change, i.e. supporting people in seeing the challenge.) Based on their new understanding, they prioritized a set of values and drivers for cultural change. The group's suggestions created a basis for decision for the management team. During this meeting the lack of trust in management became apparent and voiced. Their history showed a pattern of change initiatives not being followed through.

Step 3. Management team reflects and decides – start 'Planning the journey'

A week later, the management team met and reflected on the suggestions from the group of 30, as well as on how to address the lack of trust. They ended up with a clear decision and agreed on a way forward.

Step 4. Decision is communicated and task groups are formed – 'Planning continues'
The decision taken by management was communicated to the group of 30 a week later. Volunteers were invited to form task groups for planning and implementing the chosen change drivers, which involved leadership and co-worker training programs, new decision and information forums, etc.

Their change journey in brief
A key requirement for success was building trust in management. That required focused conversations in the management team. They needed to see how their current behavior supported a lack of long-term commitment and continuous follow-ups. Awareness of reality, of what is[11], supported real change in their behavior.

One of the chosen change drivers was regular business updates for all co-workers, where management team members took turns sharing information. This proved to be helpful in building trust in two ways. The management team became more visible, and visibility itself often creates trust. Another, even more important benefit was that meeting with the co-workers on a regular basis supported the top leaders in understanding the true meaning of being accountable.

I have yet to see resistance that is not connected to any of the sources described above. I don't believe that we resist change for the sake of resisting, nor that some people are born resistant. When we resist change we have reasons for doing so. As individuals we may have a personal history that makes certain changes, or change at a certain time, particularly challenging. It is however rarely fruitful to keep our main focus on individuals when leading change. To make informed choices of where and how to intervene in change, we get more out of noticing the forces of resistance and engagement on other levels of the system than the individual.

Having said that, of course we also need to see and cater for the needs of individuals; that is the only humane thing to do.

When we experience inertia to change

Some organizations have ingrained patterns of resistance. If you work in an organization that experiences strong inertia to change, you might recognize one or several of the following expressions of resistance:

- Low trust in leadership. People make things work despite the leaders, so when leaders initiate change people have no reason to believe that the change is for the good. Frequent head replacements or managers who often change their minds are some plausible reasons for this. It can also be that leaders are trusted only as administrators and spokespeople for their teams but have no legitimacy as change agents[12]. (The predominant source of resistance is 'I don't trust you').

- Organizations that have operated in a stable market for a very long time. Seeing the need to change daily routines that have proven successful year after year requires a loud wake-up call that people can connect to. In these organizations we can often see people rely heavily on policies and rules, which in itself can be a hindrance to change. (The predominant source of resistance being 'I don't get it'.)

- When the change demands things of us that we don't have the means to cope with, it makes sense that our 'not-liking-the-change-resistance' will be strong. Too many change initiatives lack training or coaching support to help people develop the necessary skills. There are times when the responsible thing to do is to recruit new people with the right skills. Sadly, we can sometimes see managers shying away from that responsibility and instead judge people as hopelessly resistant, letting them come to their own conclusion that they no longer have the right competence for their role.

- When change initiatives pile up and people have no means of successfully delivering on all the expectations or when goals are overly ambitious and/or timeplans are unrealistic. (Another example of 'I don't like it', or 'I don't see how I can manage the change'.)

- And lastly, a corporate culture that fears making mistakes will always say no to anything that shakes up the status quo. It could be that mistakes are punished in one way or another or, that they never even get close to making a mistake by always playing it safe. (Probably a combination of 'I don't like it' and 'I don't trust you'.)

When we get stuck in a judgmental place – judging others or ourselves as hopelessly resistant, the fact that living itself is a creative process is a soothing reminder. We are constantly emerging anew in the present moment. Our cells are being renewed every second of our lives. We are change. And we continuously affect our environment, and it affects us. It can also be helpful to know that resistance expressed by an individual may also belong to the group, or to the larger system. For some reason that person is the voice for that resistance at this moment. Something needs to be expressed.

Being brave is easier when we are not alone

Someone recently shared a quote with me: *"If you want to be a popular leader, do talk about change, but for God's sake, don't change anything!"* Unfortunately there is some truth to this. Real change is not easy, it requires a lot of determination and courage. Meaningful involvement along the way can turn potentially painful resistance into powerful energy and it leaves change leaders less alone. So, connecting what we know about change to involvement processes creates conditions for powerful, exciting, meaningful and sustainable change.

Change and involvement in Dharavi, Mumbai's largest slum

Dharavi is Mumbai's largest slum with about one million inhabitants. A while back the city planned to sell the land and, subsequently, tear the houses down. They met strong and well-organized resistance from the inhabitants of Dharavi that finally led to a stop to the selling process and the authorities are now choosing another approach. They are, in close collaboration with those living in Dharavi, improving infrastructure and sanitation. It is a sensitive process as the trust in the authorities, for good reasons, is very low. And improving living conditions in the slums without seriously involving the inhabitants would, according to anthropologist and head of the think-tank Megacities, Janice Perlsman, never work however well intentioned. Upgrading the slums, integrating them in society, is according to Perlsman the only way forward and governments need to find a way of doing that together with the poor.

Think of a change in your workplace in the recent past that affected you, yet you were not the initiator of the change. How was your own resistance/support related to the change? Did you get it? Did you like it? Did you trust the leaders of the change? And how did you express your resistance?

As you know your workplace – and yourself – in which phases would you say you are generally strong? And where do you need to put more focus?

- *Making a compelling case for change among significant stakeholders, going from being in the dark to seeing the challenge*
- *Planning the journey*
- *Moving ahead with action*
- *Staying the course*
- *Reaping the benefits*
- *Time to move on*

If you or your team is planning a major change, here are some questions to reflect upon:

- *Who are your most significant stakeholders? Who needs to be on board in order for the change to happen?*
- *How will you go about bringing the key stakeholders from being in the dark to seeing the challenge?*
- *How will you ensure that you keep key stakeholders in the loop all through the change process?*
- *When will you start reaping the benefits of the change? Are you realistic? Will you stay with the change process until then? If not, how will you make sure that someone else does?*
- *How will you stay mindful of the support and resistance present all through the change process? How is the climate for expressing resistance in your workplace?*
- *How is your own resistance to this change, and how do you deal with it?*
- *Is the change initiative you are responsible for one of many? If so, how can you help people see the big picture? And what difference would it make for succeeding with the change?*
- *How can you make fruitful use of involvement processes, using different levels of involvement, all through your change process?*

Imagine…
In your workplace, if you were to involve people in change processes to a greater extent and with more awareness, how would that impact your success rate? How would it affect your working climate? How would it impact your organization's relationship with its customers, clients, patients…

Part Two

Planning and Designing the Meeting

Immersion

"We have the most leverage on a meeting's success before any person has stepped into the meeting room".

Sandra Janoff and Marvin Weisboard[13]

Planning is key to meetings with meaning, and yet many of us tend to overlook planning. I hope to make a case for what you can gain from giving more attention to the planning phase. I will present a step-by-step approach, and in connection to each step I share a handful of tips related to different types of meetings.

Planning has both a practical and a dynamic dimension. When designing a meeting we need an understanding of what we as human beings tend to think, feel and do when we come together. And how we through respecting and making use of the way most groups behave can help a group in becoming task-focused and wise.

2.1. Six Steps to Meetings with Meaning

A step-by-step approach

A step-by-step approach helps us remember every little detail that a meaningful meeting is about. It is easy to underestimate the time needed for planning. Hopefully, by visually being reminded that there are four steps before the actual meeting we will start planning challenging meetings well in advance. It is not uncommon that the planning time for a meeting exceeds six months, though in my experience the planning starts anywhere from one to eight months before the meeting takes place.

All these steps can seem cumbersome, and of course you may browse through some of them from time to time. It all depends on the type of meeting you are planning. As is the case with many models, the steps show a sequential approach that is ideal but rarely happens in real life. Many times, people have been invited and the venue has been booked before clarifying the purpose of the meeting, and often with good reason.

The six steps to meetings with meaning
The first step – creating a strong foundation – is about two things: clarifying our reasons for having the meeting and letting participants know how much room they have to maneuver. In other words, what do we want to achieve as a direct result of the meeting as well as more long-term, and to what extent are we willing to delegate decision power to the meeting, and any other relevant boundaries.

6. Meeting Follow-up
5. Facilitating the Meeting
4. Ensuring Healthy Working Conditions
3. Designing the Meeting
2. Planning the Meeting - who to involve and invite
1. Creating the Foundation - goals and boundaries

Once we have a strong foundation for our meeting we have a fair chance of knowing who needs to be in the meeting room, which is part of step number two – the planning. Planning also involves deciding if you need to engage a professional facilitator, something that can be useful when the meeting involves a large number of people, or if it is challenging in other ways. You may also choose to assign someone to document the work and you need to consider the meeting follow-up.

Step number three – designing the meeting – is in its essence about making the most of the resources we will have in the room, that is a diverse group of engaged and competent people. What do they need to be able to do the work? A well-designed working process is as important as fresh air, natural daylight, food and refreshments – which is our fourth step, ensuring healthy working conditions.

Once people arrive to the meeting we need to support their presence and their courage to bring out the best in themselves and in each other; that's what facilitation is about – step number five.

And finally, the sixth and last step that is so easy to miss and yet so important – the meeting follow-up. Making sure that the participants are updated on what is happening as a consequence of the meeting plays a vital part in respecting their engagement in the task.

The following chapters will guide you through each step.

2.2. Creating the Foundation – The First Step

Defining compelling goals

The task-owner has an important role in this step. In order to ensure the most important preconditions for successful involvement there are a few questions that need to be answered. What are the goals or what is the purpose of the meeting? In other words, what should be accomplished by the end of the meeting? The purpose always springs from a context; it could be a pressing need, a preparation for the future or about ceasing an opportunity. Thinking in terms of dilemmas[14] can be fruitful as it helps us avoid the trap of either/or thinking.

Let us come up with ideas on how to increase efficiency while ensuring job satisfaction.

We need to find ways to increase production quality while lowering prices to our customers.

We have to become stronger in analysis and documentation related to high risk patients while keeping our humanity and presence with our patients.

It can be helpful to do a visualization experiment. See yourself at the end of the meeting you are planning – when people are about to leave the room, what has happened? What have you achieved together? Is there anything you hope will happen more long-term as an effect of what's been going on in this meeting? The answers to these questions often fall into the following two categories[15] :

Measurable, tangible goals, such as:

- Three strong ideas on how we can measure our efficiency in such a way that our patients' needs are kept front and center
- An implementation plan for project X that includes what, when, who, etc
- Within our agreed budget, define three strong cross-department projects that will improve quality of life among the elderly in our community

Less measurable, more long-term feeling or behavior-oriented goals, such as:

- As an effect of this meeting we want to see more cross-department collaboration
- We want an increased commitment to implement our change initiative
- A change of company culture towards more individual ownership and proactivity
- Higher motivation and energy in daily work
- Reduced stress in the organization
- Increased trust in management

Goals support design and focus

The measurable, tangible goals – which I call "results" – support the meeting participants in mobilizing their energy and in creating and keeping a shared focus for the meeting. The more long-term behavior-oriented goals – which I call "effects" – can guide us in designing the meeting. For example, if we are aiming for more cross-functional collaboration, we can let people work in cross-functional groups during parts of the meeting. Or if we want to see more proactivity in daily work, we can choose to create a more open agenda where people need to take charge of their own participation, and possibly also some of the content. The experience of working and relating differently during a two-day meeting can be the starting point of a new way of collaborating.

Choosing level of involvement

We need to be clear on what level of involvement we are inviting the participants to. As described in Part One, chapter 3, that depends primarily on five things: the complexity of the task, the implementation time-span, the room to influence decisions, our courage to deal with anxiety and our belief about people's ability to contribute.

Other boundaries that need to be defined

Are there other relevant boundaries or non-negotiables that need to be stated in the meeting? In other words, where is the room to maneuver? Are there certain financial or people constraints? Is it possible, or even encouraged, to question the organization, professional roles, or the vision statement?

The relevant boundaries depend of course on the task at hand and your choice of level of involvement. If the room to maneuver is too narrow it can prevent the participants from remaining fully engaged in the meeting. On the other hand, if there *are* non-negotiables, they need to be stated at the beginning of the meeting to avoid the unfortunate situation of having to intervene in the middle of a meeting to lead people onto the "right" track.

Do we really need a meeting?

There are times when thorough reflection in our first step leads us to the conclusion that there is no need for a meeting. We might realize that the core issue of concern needs to be dealt with elsewhere in the organization. Or that there is ambivalence around the task that must be handled higher up in the hierarchy before any purposeful work can be done on the matter.

Many important issues that we are facing today are both complex, urgent and controversial. Naturally they awaken ambivalence and anxiety on all hierarchical levels in an organization. It is not uncommon that leaders on the top level lack the relational capacity[16] to successfully handle the emotional aspects of truly challenging tasks. Consequently they might delegate these tasks to a change agent, a project leader or to a meeting, and people can find themselves puzzled by the extreme turbulence the issue is creating. It is like throwing a hot potato because it burns your hand, yet as it reaches mid-level in the organization there is no one to pass it on to and people with less power do the best they can to deal with it. This is rarely done deliberately, but still creates unnecessary pain within and between people in our organizations. It can be difficult to spot in time, so if you have a hunch that this is what's at play – press pause as quickly as you can.

As task-owners this is the time for an honest assessment. Do I have a genuine need for fertilizing my task with other people's thinking or do I just want to make people believe they have a say in the matter to "get them on-board"? Hand on your heart – we have all been there. Some time back I invited our children to co-create our Christmas vacation – or so I believed. Only I had underestimated how strong my own opinions were about where to celebrate Christmas, as well as forgotten how imaginative and strong-willed my children can be about Christmas holidays. And I'm ashamed to say that I didn't consider that their father, my partner, would have an opinion on the matter. In desperation I ended up giving the kids two options, to which they exclaimed: *"Mom that's not co-creating!"*

Think of a meeting you are planning. Consider the wider context of the meeting – why does it need to take place? What difference will this meeting make? Does it play a part in a larger process? Are there aspects of the issue that need to be dealt with elsewhere in the organization before a meeting with meaning can be held? Do we really need to meet?

In your mind, picture the closing half hour of the meeting. What has been achieved? What are the measurable results of the meeting? Picture the participants' faces and their body language. What are they feeling, what are they thinking? If you look further into the future, what impact can you see inside and outside the organization, as an effect of this meeting taking place?

Can you structure what you see under the headings:
Results – measurable goals achieved by the end of the meeting

Effects – more long-term desired effects, that is, more feeling or behavior-oriented goals

Imagine…
If you were clearer on what you want to achieve with your meetings, what difference would it make for the engagement in your meetings and the quality of the output – short and long term…

2.3. Planning the Meeting - The Second Step

Putting together a planning team
To stay on top of all the relevant aspects of creating a successful meeting you might need to put together a diverse planning team, or you can choose to consult people during your planning phase. Now is the time to seek their commitment to contribute.

> Creating a planning team – an example
>
> A principal at a college preparatory high school in a challenged part of a large city was not achieving the results the school aimed for. Highly engaged teachers, adequate attendance and homework support wasn't enough. The children were tired in class, and a majority of them chose the lunch meals with the least nutrients. The principal decided to mobilize the school community around the issue, including parents and others involved in the kids' welfare. He knew that this was an issue where it is easy to go wrong – others had failed before him – so he chose to put together a planning team consisting of: two teachers (math and PE), a parent and a grandmother, two students and the school counselor. Among them they had the knowledge and experience to create preconditions for a meeting with meaning.

Inviting for success
To determine who should be invited to the meeting, both types

of goals described in Part Two, chapter 2, act as guidance: results achieved by the end of the meeting as well as the more long-term desired effects. To achieve the goals, who needs to be in the meeting room? At this point it is wise to stretch our thinking; we can think in "whole system terms "[17], including internal as well as external stakeholders. Would it make sense to involve several of the organization's hierarchical levels? Do suppliers, customers or clients need to be present, or people from the local community?

Inviting "the whole system" – an example

A traditional industry was facing major problems. They quickly needed to break the silo thinking in the firm, as well as make all co-workers take leadership for their tasks. The idea came up of inviting people from all departments and from all hierarchical levels to a meeting where they were to address the situation. This might not seem very radical, but for this company it was way outside their comfort zone. And yes, they did it; the meeting was a success and proved to be the start of a new company culture.

Another way of thinking is to define what knowledge and/or experience we need in the meeting. Do people who are concerned with the outcome of the meeting need to be there? If the meeting's purpose is to create a project description for a new invoice system, maybe customers and administrative personnel need to be involved?

Don't exclude people who are far away or who for other reasons cannot attend the meeting physically as there are so many means of meeting virtually.

A pitfall to avoid is inviting people as representatives of a certain group, be it the marketing division, suppliers, teachers, or parents.

People need to participate in their own right, bringing their own voice to the meeting.[18]

It is also easy to unwarily miss, or consciously avoid, inviting people who voice resistance to the change initiative. I hope I made my point of view clear on that in the chapter on change, Part One, chapter 4.

Experts, presenters and other invitees

Some meetings require expert input in order for the meeting participants to be able to do their job. This can be tricky, as your invitees might want to share more than what is meaningful in the context of the meeting. We don't want our meeting to turn into a series of lectures, where the participants sit back and enjoy the ride. To prevent this from happening we need to be clear with the invitees on the purpose of the meeting and on their contribution to the meeting's success. We may also choose to include brief coaching sessions for invited experts and other presenters in our planning process. More on this in the next chapter, Part Two, chapter 3, where we focus on how to design the meeting.

Documenting

Documentation is easy to overlook. Do we need to give this responsibility to anyone? Again, it probably depends on the task at hand. I've been in too many meetings where this task is spontaneously thrown into someone's lap whose active participation in the meeting is consequently limited.

Facilitation

Is the meeting of such complexity or potential high tension that you need a professional facilitator to support you with the design and facilitation? Other good reasons for engaging a professional facilitator is the need for someone who is neutral in relation to the task, or simply that the task owner wants and/or needs to participate fully in the meeting. Being task-owner and facilitator in one and the same person implies many challenges. This is a good time to put your hand on your heart again – will the quality of the meeting suffer if you as task-owner facilitate it yourself? Here are some soul-searching questions:

- Is your voice needed in the work during the meeting – loud and clear?
- Are you very attached to your own ideas and opinions on the matter of concern?
- Can you expect tension due to differences of opinion or to the challenging nature of the task? Do you feel unsure of how you will handle it? Is there a risk that you will put a lid on differences or keep anxiety and tension at a minimum?

If your answer is yes to any or all of the questions above it is advisable to ask a meeting designer/facilitator for help.

Pre-contacts with participants

We are influencing the invitees' level of engagement with every communication we have with them prior to the meeting, be it e-mails, phone calls or face-to-face encounters. A dull invitation or a brusque conversation in a corridor has an impact on our meeting's success. So we need to remember to send inspiring and informative invitations, clarify our expectations, as well as distribute any needed preparation material to the participants well in advance.

The meeting follow-up

Lastly, we need to consider the follow-up. Those we involve in the meeting deserve to stay informed of how the output of the meeting is being put to use. By assigning the responsibility for meeting follow-up to someone, or to a team, we make sure that it isn't forgotten. There is more on meeting follow-up in Part Three, chapter 2, page 132.

Think of a meeting you are currently planning, who needs to be involved in the planning process?

Will any invitees be presenting during the meeting? If so, how will you brief them and how will you support them prior to the meeting?

Who needs to be present in the meeting room – virtually or face-to face – to make it possible to achieve the results and effects you are aiming for?

Do you need to ask someone to document the meeting?

Who will facilitate the meeting?

Who will formulate and send out invitations and any preparation material?

How will you ensure meaningful long-term follow-up?

Imagine…
If significantly more time was spent on the planning of meetings in your workplace, how do you think it would affect the quality of your meetings…

2.4. Designing the Meeting and Ensuring Healthy Working Conditions – The Third and Fourth Steps

Designing is, at its core, about creating the preconditions for the participants to do their absolute best to achieve the goals of the meeting. The foundation and the planning are our stepping-stones for the design phase. Designing a meeting is about making a structure, being creative and remaining flexible. A supportive design makes meetings flow organically. To experience that flow, the design needs to cater for the three phases needed in any meeting: warming up to the task and to each other, doing the work and closing the meeting.

Before we take a closer look at each of these phases I will reflect on some general aspects related to designing meetings.

Working with others and embracing anxiety

To make the most of human behavior we need to have an understanding of what we tend to do when we come together to focus on a task of shared concern. We all have this knowledge, since we are all humans and we all have been there. We just need to bring our experience of working together with others into our awareness.

We are group-beings, which is a good start for a meeting; collaborating with others is what we do. Nevertheless, if the group is new – as in not having worked together before – which is often the case in multi-stakeholder meetings, most of us start off a bit shy, sharing little of ourselves. We are normally polite and concerned with inclusion/exclusion issues. Will the others approve of me? Do I approve of them?[19] One way of going with this would be to help people get to know one another, something we rarely have time for. We have a task to accomplish, usually within a tight time frame. And the good news is that the task can help us work through our initial hesitation and shyness. We need a clear and engaging task focus before the meeting – through invitations and other precontacts. And we need to get intimate with the task early in the meeting. When we connect with something that is bigger than ourselves and of shared concern for those present, somehow our personal inhibitions are less relevant. We become more courageous in expressing ourselves – our opinions, our experience, our thoughts, our concerns, and our hopes for the future. Our ability to stay open to other's thoughts, fears and dreams also increases.

When the task matters, is larger than myself, and is of concern for all of us, it becomes possible to be passionate, confused, to agree and disagree.

It is encouraging to know that modern brain-research can measure that brain waves get synchronized when people engage in complex teamwork, such as playing a classical piece of music, or handling a business challenge. It is worth noting that a key ingredient for several brains to dance together is each person's willingness to collaborate[20].

Ambiguity, confusion and anxiety are natural parts of any meeting with meaning, *"anxiety is energy, seeking for a creative outlet"*[21]. It is an energy that is to be welcomed and embraced. This anxiety is related to at least two things – being in a (new) group of people and the importance of the task that we are here to deal with. We don't want to waste that precious energy by using an icebreaker that has no connection to the task at hand, but rather let people connect with each other through connecting with the task. However, allowing the natural anxiety is not to be confused with confusing people unnecessarily. We need to care for peoples' needs by providing a reasonably clear time and task structure. Many of us like to know what is going to happen. We want to know when we will have a break, time for ourselves, be able to make that phone call, get refreshments or have a smoke. When we know that some of our basic needs will be taken care of during the course of the meeting, we are more inclined to relax and be fully present.

Understanding our negativity bias

When designing meetings, it is helpful to keep in mind that we have a natural tendency to give more attention to negative experiences. It made sense for our ancestors as it helped them to stay alive. Neuropsychologist Rick Hanson uses a poignant metaphor when he says that our brain is like Velcro for negative experiences and like Teflon for positive. We tend to over-generalize from negative experiences and we are bad at learning from the good. Bringing this knowledge into our meeting design guides us to allocate time for focusing on opportunities as well as on what we are currently doing well. This doesn't mean that we should avoid talking about our struggles and our "sorries".

Staying true to ourselves and open to others

How can we help a group of diverse people find their individual truth moment by moment, dare to express it, not give it up at the first critical comment or lifted eyebrow, while at the same time remain open to being influenced? To combine individual reflection with focused listening in pairs, and sharing and sense making in the whole group are ways to support a deeper connection with oneself, an honest expression of our truth as well as non-judgmental listening. Finding ways to engage our physical being also supports us to "stay tuned", as our heart, our thoughts and our voice are our instruments – instruments that need to stay tuned all through the meeting.

Finding "good enough" ways of working

There are so many tools, techniques and methods available for work in large groups that it is easy to get lost. There are tools that help us enhance creativity, tools for critical thinking, tools for brainstorming and analysis, etc. Techniques, methods and tools can create a sense of false security and we may start our design process with a tool we like. The tool or technique should come last in our design process. When we have done our homework – a strong foundation – and we have an understanding of the different phases of a meeting, we will find good enough tools to use. It is also largely about personal style. There are almost no limitations to how you can work in a meeting, and very few rights and wrongs.

Here are four basic tips to start you off. For more ideas on methods, see Books Than Can Inspire on page 143.

1. Making work visible and changeable
2. Sanction playfulness
3. Variation to keep us alert and cater for individual preferences
4. The room affects us – and one room is cyberspace

1. Making work visible and changeable

For people to work efficiently in a meeting we need to find ways to make the work visible and possible to change as more data is brought in. Personally, I like using big white paper on the wall and extra sticky Post-it notes that you can move around, add to as work progresses, remove, replace and cluster when needed.

A good starting point when choosing working methods are the tools that the organization is already familiar with. Most of them can be modified for use in large groups. You can draw any four-fielder on paper on the wall and people can use Post-its for sharing their ideas. A process analysis can also be made on a wall. If you want to use computer-based tools, just make sure that the work is visible to all and that your participants can continuously add and take away data.

2. Sanction playfulness

Samuel West, who is doing research on creativity and innovation at work[22], has found that a playful attitude at work promotes openness and mental flexibility, it increases inner motivation and it builds relationships. I believe his research reinforces what we instinctively know. When we have a playful attitude to our work we get more emotionally connected with the task and with each other, which helps us talk about what really matters, what really makes a difference and what we really believe in.

When suggesting creative ways of working I sometimes encounter some concern, but I have never experienced that people don't have access to their creativity. We don't need to be in advertising or artists to be creative. Normally, once people are given permission to be playful, they throw themselves into it. I've seen managers in production industries talk about future challenges as a fairy tale, business people sharing their strategic goals in the form of a fictitious press conference, teams portraying their biggest challenges in a skit, teachers making sculptures that capture the essence of their vision, CEO's doing a business plan rap, leadership teams summarizing their commitments in a poem. And I promise, the message sticks.

A playful presentation

A department was working in cross-functional groups, searching for patterns of behavior that were holding them back. One group highlighted their poor meeting culture as one of the hindrances to success. They enacted a meeting on stage where meeting participants came late and left early, were double-booked, where some were on the phone or on their laptops, where the purpose was unclear and people came unprepared. I heard those watching whisper to each other *"this is exactly the way it is!"*. It was a big wake-up call for everyone and from what I've heard, from then on their meeting culture changed. True awareness and acknowledgement of what is often leads to change.

3. Variation to keep us alert and cater for individual preferences

Some of us are introverts and are not inclined to express our thoughts spontaneously. Others are extroverts, who speak and think at the same time. Some are more tactile in their way of making sense of things, others are more abstractly analytical. Some can think for hours, others lose focus quickly. Some come alive by arguing, and it intimidates others. The best we can do to cater for the different personalities and needs we are likely to have in the meeting room is to vary the way we work. Reflecting independently, working in pairs and smaller groups, using different tools and methods and always keeping the task front and center.

Increasing awareness by making human sculptures

They had re-designed their organization and were now to work in a Matrix[23]. Two years had passed, yet the new organizational set-up was not much more than a paper product. It had actually made matters worse. It was meant to inspire to a more holistic view, to more meaningful collaboration across traditional boundaries and a greater customer focus. Instead people felt powerless, not trusted and even paralyzed. They had talked and talked and talked about it. To get out of the deadlock I invited them to create human sculptures in the room, taking some of their struggles into account, such as closeness and distance, connections and disconnects, isolation and togetherness, leaning towards and turning away, differences and common ground, trust and mistrust, etc. Bringing their bodily awareness and wisdom into the meeting supported them to move out of the trap of intellectualizing, which in some organizations is the most widely used and accepted defense mechanism.

4. The room affects us – and one room is cyberspace

In a room with natural daylight and plenty of oxygen people are more likely to stay awake and focused. If you don't have access to that, make sure to compensate with plenty of short breaks, and keep water and fruit available. It is our job to ensure healthy working conditions.

Chairs in a circle without tables have multiple advantages. Tables help us hide more than half of our bodies, which can create a sense of security. Since we need the energy in the anxiety that facing an important challenge offers us, we don't want to reduce anxiety with tables. Another aspect is that we want to allow eye contact between all participants. Square tables, which are commonly found in conference rooms, don't allow for that to happen. Also, having no tables makes the room so much more flexible. We can easily move our chair and create a pair, or make a small group of five, and then return to conversing in the large group. And maybe most importantly, sitting in a circle is in most cultures a symbol of equality. It clearly supports us to be mindful of the whole, to not get stuck in parts. When we sit in a circle we listen more attentively, we express ourselves with more care, and we tend to make more inclusive and integrating statements. So the circle is great for finding common ground and concluding, as well as for closure. I also use the circle when starting a meeting. It helps us acknowledge and honor everyone's presence.

I prefer working in a large room with plenty of wall space, where people can work in different group constellations and document their work without using breakout rooms. Somehow, remaining in the same room supports focused and highly energized work.

More and more meetings take place in cyberspace. This can be a fantastic way of meeting, which saves traveling time, money and the environment, as well as supporting work/life balance. When planning meetings where all or some of the participants will participate on-line, the principles described in this book are even more relevant. Staying focused and energized is challenging when we rely only on listening. A clear task focus is fundamental, as are listening skills and respecting differences. To keep the energy high we need breaks more often than in face-to-face meetings. If a majority of the participants are in a meeting room and a minority participate via other media, we need to remind the "live group" that part of the group cannot see their nods, hear their humming or participate in subtle jokes. Paradoxically, this can contribute to greater honesty and frankness, since we don't get away with unclear statements or half sentences. Also, avoiding long presentations is even more important as we, especially if we don't see each other, have no good way of knowing if the listeners have checked out or not.

Ways of working together during a meeting
The number of participants influences our design. It appears that there are certain numbers of participants that require a shift in design. A group of five people doesn't ask for pair or small group work, but individual reflection can be very valuable. Six to ten people can also include meaningful work in pairs. Ten to thirty or forty[24] usually requires us to vary between individual reflection, work in pairs, triads, small group work and working in the large group. When the

group is larger than thirty or forty we need to be mindful of the work we choose to do with the whole group, as it can become tiring and boring. This includes lengthy group discussions as well as reporting small group assignments to the entire group.

When designing our meeting, here are different ways of working:

- Individually – for coming up with ideas, for reflecting and digesting
- In pairs – for sharing thoughts, exploring or discussing
- In triads with people who are likeminded or diverse
- In small groups, 4-6, likeminded or diverse
- In the large group – each person can share in a go-around, you can have open discussions, or "fish-bowl conversations", meaning that a conversation takes place in a small group for a limited time while the rest of the group is listening, the "relay" is then passed on to the next small group, etc until everyone has contributed to the conversation.

We can invite people to work standing up, walk-and-talk, or sitting down. Using a variety of physical experiments is often meaningful as well as energizing. All in all, a sound variation supports energy in our meetings.

By the way, poor working material can drain a group of energy. Make sure you have markers that work and Post-its that stick. After more than twenty years experience of conference centers I always bring my own working material, just in case. And so far it has always come in handy.

We will now connect these general aspects related to designing meetings with the three phases needed in any meeting; warming up, doing the work and closing the meeting.

Warming up – phase one

We need to warm-up, both to the task and to each other. In other words, we need to mobilize energy for working on the task at hand together with the other meeting participants. I always trust that peoples' minds are all over the place at the start of a meeting. They may be thinking of some unfinished business from the meeting they just left, or that they forgot to pack the gym clothes for their children in the morning, or the challenging performance talk they are having tomorrow[25]. The amount of stuff that is going through our minds at any given moment is endless. So we need to help people become mentally present and connected to what we are here to do, and to those we are going to do it with.

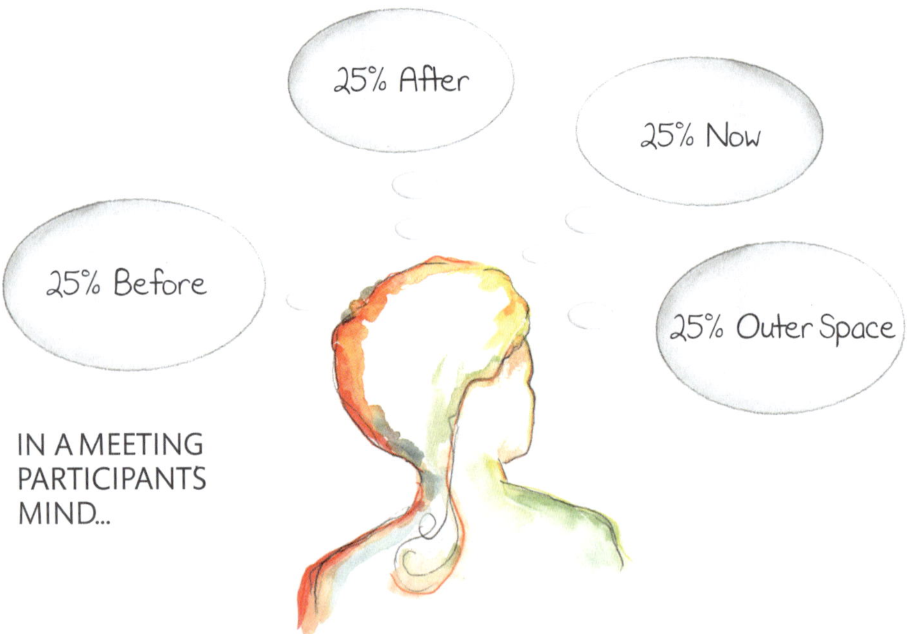

IN A MEETING PARTICIPANTS MIND...

Task introduction – a job for the task owner

The start-up includes an introduction of the task, the purpose or goals of the meeting, a brief background as to why this meeting is taking place and any relevant boundaries. This is a job for the task-owner. Connecting the task to why this particular group of people has been invited supports the participants in linking themselves and the others present to the work at hand.

Keeping the goals, any relevant boundaries and a brief agenda on flipcharts supports structure and task focus.

Avoiding input over-load

A risk at the beginning of a meeting is saying too much. There are two good reasons for avoiding this. First of all, we run the risk of not being heard, as people are in the process of becoming mentally present. Secondly, the longer we make people sit and listen, the bigger the risk of turning our meeting participants into an audience rather than a working group.

When there is a lot we need to share with the participants for them to be able to do the work, it is advisable to divide the information into two parts. Below is an example of a warm-up introduction to a four-day high stake meeting owned by the senior managers of the two concerned departments. There were twenty-two participants from the two departments. By the way, a warm-up introduction is well worth rehearsing as it sets the tone for the entire meeting.

A task introduction

Task owner/Department Head A: *"Warm welcome! I am grateful that we are all here. Some of you have traveled far, and I thank you for that. As we all know, we have struggled for years to create preconditions for a strong business."*

Task owner/Department Head B: *"Yes we have, we in Poland from our end, and you here in China from your end. And to be honest, I think that we at times have both blamed the other for our shortcomings. So it's high time we sit around the same table, with our curiosity of each other turned on. We need to explore every possible angle of our shared business before we decide on a strong action plan."*

Task owner A: *"The goal of this meeting is to have a really strong action plan when we go home to our respective countries on friday. A plan that will create a successful business, a plan we all believe in and will implement wholeheartedly. Another more long-term goal is that we, as an effect of working together these days, will create stronger, more open and trusting relationships between us. That would make us all more capable to handle any difficulties that might arise in our working process going forward. A boundary to keep in mind for this meeting is that the solutions we come up with will be within the current organizational set-up, including the number of employees we have today. And it is important that we stick to our business strategy."*

Task owner B: *"As you can see, some of us who are present in this room are decision-makers within our shared business. However, to really get to the bottom of our challenges, we also need you, our experts within new materials, sourcing and sales. So, now it's up to us to make the most of all the resources we all bring to this meeting. Before we get to work, we'd like you to reflect a bit on us being here with this task to handle. Please turn to the person sitting next to you, take a few minutes to make your own sense of what we just said. We will then hear from you all on how you experience being here. Any hopes, fears, confusions…and of course, your name and role, as we don't all know each other."*

Inviting everyone's voice

In any meeting, getting everyone's voice in the room as early as possible supports individual engagement and sense of responsibility for the work. So letting participants reflect on the introduction, either individually or in smaller groups, depending on the number of participants in the meeting, is a good way to instill energy and engagement. A metaphor that makes sense to me is the philharmonic orchestra that tunes their instruments as the audience is taking their seats. Since our voices, as well as our minds and hearts, are our instruments, they need some tuning, tuning into ourselves as well as to one another.

Process introduction – a job for the facilitator

Sharing the rationale for the design, or how we will work during the course of the meeting, in combination with suggesting a conducive stance or attitude is helpful. In the event you are working with a professional facilitator, this is the time to hand over to that person.

A process introduction

Task owner: *"As I want and need to participate fully in our work I have invited an experienced facilitator to guide us through these days. I will now hand over to..."*

Facilitator: *"My job as your facilitator is to create the conditions necessary for you to do your best at achieving the goals of this meeting.*

I'd like to say a few words about how we will work together and why. You've just started to get connected with the task, as well as with each other. We will soon move on to explore challenge X, Y and Z from different perspectives so that you can get a fuller picture of the issue.

Based on that picture you will define the key drivers for change and dig deeper into those in smaller groups, Each group will then share their understanding of each change driver, as well as their suggested actions, with the whole group. You will give each other feedback on your ideas, and then conclude.

As you can see there's a plan, a design, but we will continually evaluate and adjust as needed. A rough agenda with starting, ending, break, lunch and dinner times is on the wall.

Lastly, to make the most of the diversity you bring to this meeting we can be inspired by the words curiosity and suspending judgment..."

As meeting facilitators we all have our own style. For some for us, it comes naturally to tell a story that illustrates something of relevance for the meeting. Others might choose to elaborate around a meaningful quotation, or play a piece of music with a relevant beat or meaningful lyrics. When you want something different to happen, starting the meeting with something novel helps.

Supporting shared responsibility

If it is a high stake meeting and you want to help people connect with their sense of responsibility for the outcome, you can invite the group to reflect on questions such as: *What is the best that we can make happen during this meeting? What is the worst that we can make happen?*[26] And then ask them to summarize their thoughts on Post-it notes and put them in two columns on the wall. This wall can act as a reminder and inspiration throughout the meeting. It can also be a useful point of reference for the group's self-evaluation when closing the meeting.

The best and the worst we can make happen

This is a list of 'the best and worst' made by a group of forty leaders as they met for two days to work on their business direction. The meeting took place early in their work with the new direction. On top of supporting the participants to warm-up to the task and to each other, it helped them get connected with their own responsibility for successful change. These wants and dreads can also be read as a checklist of what is needed from leaders for real change to happen – and how we can stop change from happening.

(By the way, this organization ended up with a strong and radical direction, largely as a result of using meaningful involvement all through the working process. And simultaneously, they created preconditions for successful implementation.)

This is the BEST we can make happen these days…

Mobilize the courage to make drastic change & brave unity to do it!
Decisions and actions
See and feel the result of our involvement
A customer-focused mission and vision
We find the key to our future success
Shared responsibility for OUR future
A mission to change the world - that motivates and attracts people
Know how to involve our co-workers
Connect the change/future with what's actually working today
Connecting with our emotions
Common understanding, but maybe not agreement – on where we are heading
Open and constructive atmosphere

This is the WORST we can make happen…

"Somebody else can fix this"
Stuck in details
Defending what is = not challenging enough
Confusion and ambiguity
Pockets of silent resistance
Little understanding of the need for change and sense of urgency
Not feeling safe in involving my co-workers in the new direction
We pretend to agree – false consensus
No shared vision – a split vision
We leave like silos, without having understood each other
Ideas on change not big enough
Not being open and honest
Not being concrete enough – just a lot of talking

Brief and engaging input
When the meeting requires knowledge sharing or updating the participants about certain preconditions, this is often part of the warm-up. Giving any kind of input from experts, or others, can be a challenging part of the planning process. From our perspective as meeting owners and facilitators, we want to avoid lengthy input since that will put the participants in "being-fed-mode". And there is the experts' or presenters' perspective. They may have a lot to share that they believe would benefit the participants and the quality of the meeting. This can become a tricky negotiation. As meeting owners and facilitators we need to keep the goals in sight, as well as honor what we know about meeting dynamics, and communicate that to the presenters. We can also try to influence the quality of the presentations. Sometimes, just banning PowerPoint and giving a clear and challenging time limit is enough to spark the presenters' creativity. We can also include support to presenters in our planning process, and a "dry run" before the actual meeting.

Highly engaging short presentations

They gathered the entire company to create shared meaning of key aspects of their business plan, as well as to agree on some first important steps towards successfully delivering on the plan. The meeting's planning team had, after passionate conversations, decided on the focus and realized that it required some highly engaging short presentations – no longer than 10 minutes each. These presentations were to be made by people working close to the tasks, not by managers.

The instructions to the presenters were: *"Make a "right-brain"- i.e. creative - presentation of maximum 10 minutes that will really help your point get across to the 120 participants."* They were also offered two "speed-coaching" sessions with the facilitator for support and inspiration. The presentations turned out great, helping the meeting participants to connect both cognitively and emotionally to their business plan.

Before stepping into phase two, 'doing the work', it usually makes sense to end the warm-up with a break, which gives people time to further digest the purpose of the meeting and informally connect with the other participants.

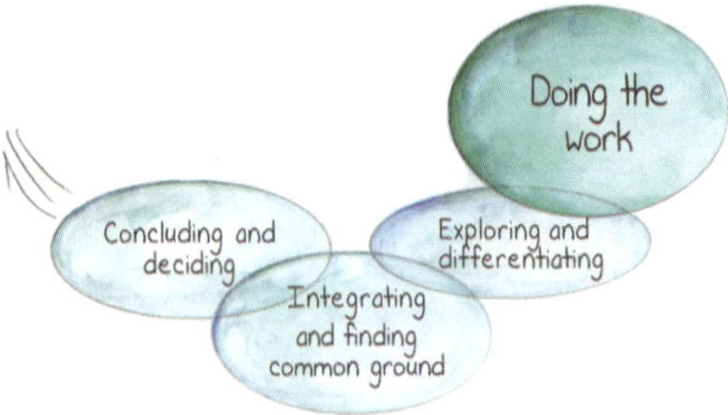

Doing the work – phase two

One of the most common pitfalls in meetings is to jump into problem solving. Consequently we end up defining what is urgent to deal with, as well as our action plans, based on a limited view of reality. The beauty of having a diverse group of people in the room is that we get a fuller picture of the context in which the issues we need to address emerge with brighter clarity. Decisions almost make themselves when we engage in courageous and honest exploration. It might sound a bit idealistic, but it works. So now is the time to make the most of a diverse group of people coming together, using the group's resources wisely and creatively.

Supporting exploring and differentiating

Exploring/differentiating and finding common ground are two very different processes that require different states of mind. When we explore and differentiate we need an open mind; we need to both slow down and speed up our thinking, and we rely on our curiosity and our courage to express our thoughts, feelings and opinions. By staying in exploration a little longer than we think we need, we get wiser together, and the next step, integrating ideas and finding common ground, becomes a lot easier.

Doing the work – from differentiating to finding common ground

The purpose of a three-day meeting was to leave with an action plan that would ensure business success. After the warm-up phase, which included some business and people updates, they began 'doing the work' by differentiating. This was done as follows:

Facilitator:
"Based on what you've heard and learned so far about your business, your customers, your people and yourselves – you are now to unearth your core challenges. You will do this in three steps to support differentiation and then you will integrate and find common ground.

Step 1.
Two and two, where one of you listens to the other's thoughts on: What do you see as your core challenges? Three minutes, then I will ask you to change roles; from listener to speaker and vice versa. You will get to change speaking partner two to three times, so that you get a chance to fertilize one another's thinking.

Step 2.
Based on your individual findings, we will make a group mind-map on the wall, i.e. move to searching for common ground. You might find a pattern, interesting polarities, intriguing contradictions… we will see.

Step 3.
With the support of certain criteria, you will then prioritize your three core challenges.

As for the next step you will, based on the three core challenges, define what needs to change, with clear actions and responsibilities. The working method we will use for that is called "carousels", as you will move around, working on all three challenges in three corners of this room. You will divide into three groups, connected to your different responsibilities in the business. The groups will move clock-wise, spend one hour in each working corner, start and end in the corner with the challenge you are responsible for. One person in each group needs to remain with "your" challenge all through the process to be able to pass on any relevant information. All work should be documented, using the material available – flip charts,

Post-its, markers, etc. Your job in this working carousel is to challenge and support each other to see and acknowledge whatever needs to be seen and acknowledged. At 2 pm each working group will have about 45 minutes to share their work with the whole group.

Meeting owner:
"Our next step is to make clear commitments – which we will do tomorrow morning, as we trust that sleeping on our discoveries will support us in making a plan we truly believe in."

True differentiation, where problem solving is put on hold, is a new experience for many people. There is often a magic moment, or several, during this phase. Sometimes experienced as an aha – as in, *"I've never understood the full complexity of this matter before"*, sometimes as a big relief, *"I have felt so alone with this issue, sharing this picture with you lifts a ton of weight from my shoulders"*. At times it makes people realize that they have been digging in the completely wrong place, *"now we see what this is really about"*, which is not always a pleasant experience. It can include guilt and grief but also relief and joy. We cannot make magic moments happen, though we can create a design that makes them possible. And we can cultivate our sensitivity to notice magic moments, as well as help the group savor them when they do happen.

Exploring differences is an unusual and untried strategy for most of us. It's about giving up certainty in favor of the unknown.[27]

When choosing methods for exploring it makes sense to use tools that are known to your organization. If people are familiar with SWOT analysis[28] you can do a group-SWOT. Or if your organization works with Lean, Six Sigma or any other management approach for process improvement, maybe some of the tools that these approaches offer are helpful for the task you are exploring. Just enlarge it and make it workable on a wall, to make the work visible and accessible to all. Brainstorming, i.e. a free flow of ideas, can often be combined with other techniques and tools.

A Group SWOT

This company was working on its new direction. Recently a number of leaders in top management had been replaced which made it possible to challenge old truths, something they were in great need of. The management team members knew this but they were worried that the other managers would keep challenging ideas to themselves, or only share them in "corridor conversations".

In the meeting introduction the task owner, and CEO, shared his fear that the participants would hold back challenging information. To further support transparency they worked with a SWOT-analysis in several steps - from individual reflection to whole group conversations. They drew a large four-fielder on the wall and it was agreed that whenever an opinion, thought or idea had been glued to the wall it no longer belonged to the peron who wrote it, but to the whole group[29]. This agreement further supported a courageous and open exchange of thoughts, opinions and creative ideas.

Analyzing our business – step by step

1. Individual reflection – what strengths, weaknesses, opportunities and threats do you see?
2. Interviews in pairs – what do you see as our core strengths? Our

main weaknesses, our opportunities and threats.
3. Each person writes their thoughts on Post-its and puts them on the wall
4. Invite the group to sort and cluster the Post-its
5. Reflect on the findings in small cross-functional groups
6. Reflect and conclude in the large group

During dinner the participants were invited to share "our company's biggest challenge" in a creative way. The only limitation was four minutes per group. It was fun, it was honest, it was a wake-up call – and it was remembered.

Sharing group work with the large group

Presenting work done in smaller groups to the large group involves certain risks that we need to be aware of. The content may be highly interesting and important, but we can only take in so much. Boring people is never helpful, so firstly we need to ask ourselves – if or why sharing the work is needed. If it is needed and we have many subgroups presenting, we may consider optional ways of sharing. We can remix the groups, which makes it possible to share the work in smaller group constellations. Or we could opt for some kind of creative presentations, such as skits, storytelling or the like. Or people can present in the form of an art showroom or exhibition.

Searching for common ground

After exploring and differentiating we move on to integrating and searching for common ground. I like Janoff's and Weisboard's definition of common ground : *"Common Ground is real agreement at a point in time, which includes where we disagree."*[30] This way of defining common ground makes people lower their shoulders, and you can sense a sigh of relief in the meeting room. Knowing that we don't need to agree relaxes us, and helps us overcome our resistance to agree. I have learned from Weisboard and Janoff that the 80/20 rule also applies to meetings. They claim that we often tend to focus 80% of our energy on the 20% of the issues where we disagree, and suggest we do the opposite, i.e. focus 80% of our energy on the 80% where we can agree and let go of the rest. Regardless of the percentages, knowing where there is support for shared action and where there is not helps us make informed decisions for our future.

How we divide the participants into smaller working groups is of course dependent on the task and your goals. While exploring normally involves working in groups with similar perspectives, integrating and searching for common ground is often done in mixed groups. Below is an example of how this can be done and its benefits.

From differentiating to finding common ground

They met to find actions that would put a stop to fires being set off in public schools in a small community. Among the participants were students, parents, teachers, social workers, police and the local fire brigade. To clarify their different perspectives on the issue, they had spent time exploring the situation and its implications in smaller homogenous group; a parent group, a teacher group, etc. These small "like-minded" groups had shared their thoughts in the large group. (Calling a group "like-minded" does not imply that all individuals in the group share the same views, only that they have something in common that is relevant for what is being explored.)

Now was the time to integrate and search for common ground. To keep the different voices strong, pairs from the different "like-minded" groups (police, students, parents etc) joined with pairs from another group to focus on finding concerns they shared, as well as clarifying their differences.

Concluding and deciding

Then is the time to conclude and/or decide, which may involve prioritization processes and even voting. Meetings where decisions are to be made, i.e. the higher levels of involvement, are faced with a quite existential endeavor. Making decisions means saying yes to some things, and thereby saying no to something else. Many teams, including management teams, never learn to fruitfully deal with the anxiety that decision-making creates. Consequently decisions are in reality often made by a single person. Even when the official story is that they are made in a management team, or similar.

Teams can appear decisive through their ability to say yes, ticking off action lists like nothing else, and at the same time lack skills to care for the other side of the coin – saying no. This is a sure way to prevent successful change.

Concluding and Deciding

A management team was planning an important and contoversial meeting. They met for a day to define all the aspects of steps one and two – creating a strong foundation and deciding who to involve and invite. This team had very little experience of fruitful teamwork, and virtually no experience of collective decision-making. We had one day at our disposal. During the morning they explored the background from which the need for the planned meeting had emerged. And in the afternoon they decided on goals, boundaries, etc. We completed the task much earlier than the decided upon ending of the day. They were all mesmerized by the swiftness of their decision-making, asking what kind of magic wand I had used to make it happen. As I see it, the magic wand was to clearly separate the work – first exploring, then integrating/searching for common ground and lastly, deciding.

Closing the meeting – phase three

Never skimping on closure

The last phase is so important and yet often overlooked, sometimes due to lack of time. My advice is to never skimp on closure. It is better to cut the working phase short, even if it means that you need to meet again or that a smaller group needs to take on whatever remains to be done. It is in the closing part that our energy cycle can come to completion. It is a place of satisfaction and rest. And we minimize the risk of people leaving the meeting room with a lot of unfinished business, things that might drain them, and subsequently our project, of energy.

Closing has two parts, a task focus and a process or interpersonal focus. We connect back to the goals of the meeting; we clarify the next steps and possible feedback loops. We then let our participants reflect on their experience of working together, and share that with each other.

Closing the Meeting

Task owner: *"We've now come to the last part of this meeting, the ending. Let's go back to the goals. I think we can agree that we have achieved most of them? We have a draft "desired position" that needs a bit of polishing by our communication department. I'd like a few of us to take part in the polishing to make sure that the essence of our discussions here will be incorporated in the final wording of our desired position. Who would like to join?"*

And we have defined four strong change drivers. We said three to five, so we're on target there. I appreciate the open disagreements we had on the change-drivers; that really made us take a big step forward.

My concern is how we can make sure that we all stay updated on how things are moving since many of us won't experience the result of our work here for years to come. I'll take that on as my responsibility, but I will need your support.

To close, I'd like to hear a few words from each of you, anything you'd like to say in order to leave this meeting with a sense of integrity. We have about 20 minutes for this and we are 30 people here so it's less than a minute per person. To support our focus, both in listening and in speaking I will pass this talking stick[31] *around the room."*

From warming up to closing

To get an idea of what a design might look like, from beginning to end, using the model 'phases in a meeting'[32] as our framework, you can take a look at the design below. A group of leaders were responsible for leading a major change initiative. To support themselves in "being the transformation", they chose to regularly dedicate time to being, reflecting and learning together, supported by a facilitator. Below is the design for their first two-day meeting.

A Meeting Design – "Leading and being the transformation"

Goals for the first two days:

Shared understanding of our need to change, agree on our role in key change projects, evaluate our current value statement, and have a starting point for our individual development related to leading our change.

Preparing the conference room:
Food for thought on the walls, quotes connected to the meeting's focus. Ten different flowers, symbolizing the beauty of a diverse group.

Day one
WARMING UP – *To the task and to each other*
The CEO describes why this process is needed, connecting to the company's direction and a personal experience of leading transformative change, its ups and downs.
Hands over to facilitator who informs about her role, and invites the team to check in by responding/reacting to the introduction and the quotes on the wall. Facilitator shares the intended design and its rationale.

To inspire differentiation and curiosity with oneself and one another, in alternating pairs, explore the following questions:

- In relation to what we are here to focus on and our role as the leading team… where are you coming from, and what do you bring with you?
- What are your highest aspirations – what do you want to leave with tomorrow afternoon? For yourself? For us? And how can we together make that happen?
- What would be the worst that we could make happen these days?

Then share and reflect together in the whole group.

DOING THE WORK – *Differentiating and integrating*
Learning from the past – Individually reflect on your journey with the company, its ups and downs, connected to five system levels: Society, the company, the management team, my department/business and me. *(A differentiating process.)*
Transfer your journey to a long piece of paper on the wall using

illustrations, pictures and symbols. Reflect on the shared stories this communicates. What do we learn about us and our change journey? *(An integrating process)*

Interdependence – Getting a physical and direct experience of what being interdependent means by using bouncing balls. Reflect and connect the experience to your reality.

About change – Presenting theory, models and a vocabulary. Reflect, discuss and connect to your reality.

Dinner & evening work – **stories you want to tell in three years** – guided visualization and sharing. Use the night to digest the work, be ready to conclude and decide tomorrow.

Day two
Start the day with reflecting on day one.

CONTINUE DOING THE WORK – *concluding & deciding*
-Learning from the past for the future, conclude.
-Assess value statement in light of what you've learned. Alterations?
-Leadership support to key change projects?

Individual development needs and support available.
Reflecting individually, asking for and receiving feedback. Give a structure for going deeper, next step, share support structure that is available (individual coaching, 360 feedback, etc.).

CLOSING – *task and process*
- Task-owner connects back to the long-term ambition and this meeting's goals.
- Reflect back to individual aspirations with these two days.
- Individual and team commitments going forward.

Think of a meeting you are planning, how do you want to design it?

The 'warm-up' phase, to the task and to each other?

The 'doing the work' phase? Depending on the character of your meeting and the people you will have in the room, how will you help people:

- *Explore and differentiate?*
- *Integrate their thoughts and find common ground?*
- *Conclude, and possibly prioritize and decide?*

The 'closing' phase? How will you help people connect back to the goals? How will you share the next steps? How will you support people to digest and close this experience on individual and group level?

Are there any of the phases you find more challenging to design? What might be your concerns? *(See template on p.148)*

How will you ensure healthy working conditions for your meeting?

Imagine...
If you spend more time on designing the meetings you are planning, what difference would it make for the outcome of your meetings...

Part Three

Facilitating the Meeting and Meeting Follow-up

Infusion

The kind of meeting I am talking about is the one which I enter with the willingness to emerge a slightly different person.

Theodor Zeldin[33]

How can we as facilitators create an atmosphere where people are willing to influence and be influenced, where people can listen with a minimum of judgment and speak with a minimum of fear? How can we create an environment where people are curious about and use their differences; where they allow themselves to be surprised, confused, and inspired, where they learn and develop as people as they develop their business? Does it sound like a bit too much to ask from a facilitator? Maybe, and yet that is pretty much what we are asked to do. This part of the book aims to help you on the way. It also discusses the importance of meeting follow-up, how you can honor the meeting participants' engagement after the meeting has taken place.

3.1. Facilitating the Meeting

Excitement and concerns

Witnessing a diverse group of people immersed in a task of shared concern, oblivious of you the facilitator, is pure joy. Creating the conditions for that to happen is sort of like preparing the house for receiving friends you long for. Maybe you put tulips by their bedside because you know it is their favorite flower. You might air out the guest room and put fresh bed linen on the bed. You make space for their shoes and coats, and you have cleared your desk and your head to be present with your friends. Maybe this is far from what normally happens when you have friends over – I know it is for me. But I must admit that it would be nice if I were the longed for friend.

For many who lead meetings there are a lot of "what-ifs" that stand in the way of being excited about facilitating a meeting. So let's get on with the things we all, or many of us, dread and see how we can connect our concerns with the excitement of supporting a group of people in doing their job.

Common concerns

Here are some of the most common concerns I meet in others and in myself when it comes to facilitating a meeting:

What if the meeting participants don't want to be there? Or if they don't show up? Or if they leave early? Or if they don't stay focused? What if there's a bad atmosphere? Or if unresolved conflicts surface?

Or irresolvable conflicts emerge?
What if a few people dominate the meeting? Or no one talks?
What if they come up with bad ideas or poor action plans?
What if their conversations derail?
What if the hierarchy is played out in the meeting? What if no one dares to speak their mind in the presence of a senior person, or in my presence?
What if there is a disagreement in the group and I, as the facilitator and task-owner strongly agree with one side?
What if they all turn against me?

WHAT IF...

The truth is that to a certain degree, pretty much all of the above is likely to happen and the key is not to act on everything that happens, which for many of us is a real challenge. In this chapter I will present six principles that I hope will help you see what "non-action" can look like, and its benefits.

Just a word on the first concern, which is one that we can do something about. *"What if they don't want to participate in the meeting?"*. If we do our homework, steps one to four, it is unlikely that this will happen, unless we have misjudged people's time constraints or their stress levels. The task might be crystal clear, the boundaries as well; we have the right participants in the room and they are highly engaged in the task. But they are overworked, or we scheduled the meeting at the busiest time of the year, or a natural disaster happened yesterday that has an impact on our business and/or our people. If this is the case, you might consider saying *thank you for showing up, now go back to work.* Or you could reframe your task to something meaningful that can be done in two hours rather than two days. By showing that kind of respect to your participants you will probably increase their trust in you.

However, there are situations when you think the work has been thoroughly done in steps one and two – 'creating the foundation' and 'planning the meeting' – yet as the meeting begins you get a strong hunch that you are mistaken. If this happens, you are probably a professional facilitator and not the task owner. When you have a strong working alliance with your assignor/the meeting and task owner, you can consult with him or her on how to proceed. If not, I am afraid you might have to suffer through facilitating an *"as-if"* meeting. And that hurts. Hopefully it will mature into a rich experience. You might learn to ask better questions to your assignor next time to decrease the likelihood of this happening again. Or maybe you learn to say no to certain assignments. And when it does happen again, despite what you learned, just remember that you are not alone.

A personal learning experience

I was contracted by a project leader to facilitate a meeting. The project's two assignors took part in the meeting. I wasn't aware of the "never voiced disagreements" between the assignors, disagreements that proved to have a big impact on the meeting. Due to the high stake nature of the task there was a lot of potential face to be lost. Combining a weak working alliance with my assignor – the project leader – with a seemingly weak alliance between the project leader and the assignors and low trust between the assignors, this meeting was clearly risking failure. What did I do? Not much. What did I learn? To ask pertinent questions early in the process and say no to assignments that don't give the meeting participants preconditions to succeed. Do I live by what I learned? Not always. This was clearly a case of ambivalence that needed to be handled higher up in the hierarchy, which I spoke of in Part Two, chapter 2.

Let's return to the challenges you are likely to meet when facilitating, and possible ways of dealing with them. Reflecting on our role as facilitators is helpful. Janoff and Weisboard have created a quiz for facilitators that beautifully describes the dilemma between what we would like to control and what is actually within our power to control.

Quiz for facilitators[34]

Q: – What would you like to control?
A: – People's behavior, commitment, motivation, and outcomes.

Q: – What can you control?
A: – Structure.

Q: – Anything else?
A: – My own behavior?

Q: – What do you have to let go of?
A: – Controlling others' behavior, commitment, motivation and outcomes.

Q: – Why?
A: – We can't do it, and we get better results by not trying.

Six supporting principles

Here are six simple and powerful principles to hold on to when you are in a facilitating role.

Principle number one
– Create a safe emergency[35]

We have an urgent task to accomplish. Getting that sense of emergency across to the participants helps them mobilize energy for the work. At the same time, to take risks people need to feel safe enough and we need them to be risk takers for creative collaboration to happen. It is risky to question the status quo. It is risky to say something that has never been expressed. It is risky to put our much-cherished assumptions to the side, allowing ourselves to be questioned; it is risky to show our uncertainty. When we are genuinely engaged, we are both powerful and vulnerable. As facilitators we have the power to create that safe enough place, not too safe, but safe enough for people to stay curious and engaged. We do it by being in the present moment, by role modeling listening, by suspending judgment, by being curious, by respecting each person as they are, by validating their opinions; we do this by respecting the task and the goals, as well as starting times, ending times and breaks.

We also create that safe emergency by preparing the meeting room. What do we want the participants to feel and think as they enter the room? To have the purpose projected on the wall supports focus. Making something novel or thought-provoking visible in the room creates curiosity. Playing music can help people connect with themselves and make them feel at ease. Chairs in a circle without tables are in most organizations a novel feature, though not always calming as it can remind people of AA-meetings or group therapy sessions. All this fixing before anyone has arrived helps to create a safe enough place for me as facilitator as well. I have a few other ways to calm my stage fright, such as welcoming each participant personally. This usually works both ways, what makes us as facilitators feel safe enough also helps the participants. The 'warming up' phase of the meeting aims at supporting all present to sense a 'safe emergency' and be eager to get to work. If we only communicate the emergency but no sense of safety is created, people shut down. This makes sense as our primal drive is survival. That survival can be physical, as when meetings are held in war zones or during natural disasters, and it can be psychological. As task-owners our mere presence can create insecurity. If we belong to the higher levels of the hierarchy we might need to remind ourselves of the things that could be going through the participants' minds. *Will I be judged? Will my performance affect my career, etc.?*

To be able to create this safe emergency it is helpful to know that there are moments in meetings that can make a task-owner/facilitator particularly shaky. When we shiver the participants shiver too. One of those moments is the moment of truth, when a decision is about to be made in the group. It can be a slow and frustrating moment. Whatever you do, don't fall into the trap of judging the group as incapable of deciding, and as a consequence you make the decision yourself. That is changing the level of involvement in the midst of a meeting and it is extremely unproductive for people's engagement and sense of safety. Being dissatisfied with the quality of ideas can also make us nervous, and potentially critical. Just remind yourself that you have the right people in the room; honestly share your thoughts and let them go at it again. Whatever you do, don't pretend to be task neutral when you are not. Keeping a hidden agenda is a recipe for unproductive anxiety.

When a 'safe emergency' ceased to be

A project leader responsible for a new business initiative had gathered some highly engaged people to outline a plan. The project's sponsor was the former CEO, who had recently been replaced. Nothing was formally changed regarding the initiative. A day and a half into the meeting, after some courageous exploration, the walls were pasted with creative ideas and the group was moving into 'integrating and searching for common ground'. The sense of pride and excitement was tangible. At this moment the new CEO entered the room – uninvited. She looked at the walls, and started to criticize what she saw. The meeting participants went from pride to shame in a second. At this moment this meeting died – and so did the business initiative. Of course the CEO had the right to kill the idea, and doing it in the midst of a meeting with highly engaged people was certainly effective – but also painful. This initiative was never mentioned again, except in a very low voice. Yet, the pain its closure caused took years to heal. Fear and shame is highly contagious and spreads quickly in an organization.

Praising the participants can be equally unproductive. It is tempting at times, since it may reduce anxiety as well as make people like us. The downside is that we, by taking on the role of assessing the quality of work and/or people's behavior, create a group that is dependent on the leader. We want independent thinkers who take responsibility for the task together with the other meeting participants. It is much more productive to ask the participants to evaluate their work. If you started your meeting with asking the group to define the best and the worst they can make happen (see Part Two, chapter 4), the participants have, in combination with the goals of the meeting, good points of reference for self-evaluations.

Creating a 'safe emergency' by tolerating anxiety

Four hundred leaders were 'warming up to the task and to each other'. Anxiety was present. It was visible in the way people approached one another, they were tentative physically and verbally. The meeting owner approached me, sharing his concern that people might be bored, that the level of energy was too low. This is a hook to avoid getting caught on. If we interfere in this phase we stop the transformation of anxious energy into responsibility and sense of urgency. We need to rely on our design for handling this phase and trust the process. If the meeting owner trusts us, it's likely that we can convey some of our trust in the process to him or her. If not, the meeting owner might intervene, and then anything can happen.

Principle number two – Stay out of fixing people as well as fixing for people

One of our biggest pitfalls as facilitators is to think that we need to fix everything. In fact, the fixing itself has a tendency to increase whatever we are trying to fix. If we try to make dominant people shut up they are likely to speak more. If we stop an argument at the wrong moment, the group's energy and focus might get stuck in what we don't allow them to talk about. If I try to make someone – or the whole group – understand that whatever they are angry with me for really isn't my fault, it doesn't lessen people's frustration.

When we have a solid base, having worked through each step towards a meeting with meaning, it becomes a lot easier to stay out of fixing. Yet sometimes we haven't done our homework, and when that is the case we might try to compensate for our poor planning all through the meeting, which isn't very helpful. It could be that someone projects frustrations related to a challenging task onto the useless markers you have provided, or that you haven't given them enough time to complete a task. After admitting your neglect to the group, insufficient planning can be used as an opportunity to invite the group in the present moment to create whatever preconditions they need to proceed with the work.

In a meeting there are plenty of small chores and decisions, such as forming small working groups, bringing the material needed for accomplishing a task, deciding how and who to present a piece of work to the large group, etc. These things can seem insignificant and time consuming, and therefore should be handled by the facilitator or an administrator. However, the more responsibility for these smaller tasks that we delegate to the meeting participants, the more responsibility they will take for working on the issue of concern. It is as if the sense of responsibility they mobilize when getting the Post-it notes they need gets projected onto the task at hand.

Delegating responsibility to the meeting participants

Facilitator: *"You will work on this task in groups of four or five where you need a mix of people from marketing and sales. We want you to record your work on flipchart paper, which is available here. It can be helpful for your work to assign roles, such as timekeeper, presenter, note taker, and discussion leader – someone who helps the group stay on task and makes sure everyone who wants to speak gets to do so within the time allotted*[36]*. If there's any confusion, or if you need anything, I will be available in this room."*

When we do the opposite, fixing and helping too much, participants can get too comfortable and subsequently the energy drops. If you don't believe me, give it a try and you might be surprised. Nature doesn't like vacuums, so if you do less, the participants will do more[37].

Principle number three – Focus on the boundaries: task, time and method

So rather than fixing for people we should focus on clarifying boundaries. When you put people to work, be super clear about the task, how much time they have to complete it and if there is a certain method you want them to use for doing the work. When do you want people to be back, what are they expected to present and how much time is allocated for each group's presentation? We might say: *Is it clear to everyone what you are expected to do?* And if the answer is a chorus of no, or their body language signals confusion, we give it another go and rephrase our instructions.

Focusing on boundaries also involves respecting starting, ending and break times. It is about caring for people's needs – physical, practical and mental. When we don't, we run two risks: firstly, people's minds start wandering off; waiting for the break they were promised. They could be thinking of the phone call they planned to make during the break or they might just need food and drink regularly to function. Secondly, if people don't feel respected they can lose interest in the task and in each other. Openly or in their minds they might blame the facilitator – and rightly so.

Principle number four
Stay loyal to the task – it's your best friend

Another way to define our task as facilitators is that of keeping the task front and center. The beauty of this is that it works in two ways. A clear task focus helps the group to mobilize their energy and focus, and our loyalty to the task helps us when we get lost as facilitators. See the task as your best friend. If tension rises, we can ask ourselves how this tension can contribute to the work. If conversations seem to wander off, a way to help the group back on track is to remind them of the task.

The challenge of handling dominating people is often resolved by our choice of working methods. A mix of working independently, in pairs, in triads, in small groups and in the whole group gives everyone space and time to connect with themselves, mobilize the courage to share their thoughts and influence others, as well as use their curiosity and willingness to hear others out and be influenced. Should it occur that one or a couple of people dominate the conversation, you could say: *For the benefit of task X I'd like to invite some more voices into the room. Or, we hear that there are some strong opinions on X, is there anyone who would like to offer an alternative perspective on this issue?*

As facilitators we can only intervene when working in the large group; when people work in smaller constellations, we leave them alone. Yet, by modeling a respectful and task-focused way of intervening we inspire the participants to do likewise in their breakout groups.

Principle number five
Feet on the ground – and breathe – before acting

No one knows you like you, so self-reflection is a good start for finding out more about your trigger points. Do you feel uneasy when there is silence in a group? Do you jump when tension rises, or when someone seems to get their feelings hurt? Does being criticized provoke you, or do you lose your ground when you are being praised? In challenging meetings, the group works through a change process which inevitably involves awkward silence, tension, confusion, anxiety and disagreements, as well as excitement and joy. Knowing and trusting that anxiety is an energy that is seeking a creative outlet is soothing for facilitators. This is a good time to put our feet on the ground and breathe. If we intervene as soon as tension rises we prevent the needed change from happening. We need to remember that in a two-day meeting with meaning you can go through a change process with your participants that would otherwise take months. And we know that there are powerful forces at play in change. For a deeper appreciation of what change entails, see Part One, chapter 4.

Our best self-support when tension rises is our breathing. When we get nervous we either stop breathing or our breath becomes shallow, which makes creative thinking difficult. So be aware of your feet on the ground, notice and follow your breath, then think, and lastly act – if you still see a need to.

When breathing was useful

This team of about 20 had redesigned their way of working together, yet there was some non-voiced resistance that was holding them back. Their manager opened the meeting and handed over to me, the facilitator.

I was saying something about the design of the day and what I thought it would take from the group to get the job done, when a man sitting opposite me at the end of a U-shaped table brusquely stood up and left the room. I noticed a reaction among those close to him, while the people sitting on the sides seemed oblivious of the drama that was going on. I reminded myself to keep my feet on the ground, breathe, and think. I chose not to act. I put trust in my design and continued to speak. It proved to be the right thing to do this time, as he came back a couple of hours later, participated actively for the rest of the day and in the closing reflections shared this:

"We have been struggling with our collaboration for so long, painful power struggles and a lack of mutual respect. So I have to admit, I was very skeptical that this meeting would make any difference. And when you (pointing at me) got started with that crap around 'the warming up phase, and that conversations require us to suspend judgment and speak without fear…', I thought it was just too ironic. I now realize that working this way made sense, and I trust in us taking this forward. Thank you all."

However, there are times when intervening is the only responsible thing to do. When a group is paralyzed and stops working, it is our job to support them out of the paralysis. These are some of the more challenging moments for facilitators. I owe much of what I know about when and how to intervene to Sandra Janoff and Marvin Weisboard. For example, when we sense that someone is putting himself or herself at risk of being isolated or excluded from the group we need to intervene. The way we know it is happening is that someone expresses something that is highly emotionally charged and there is a gasp in the room, followed by silence. Not one of those juicy silences that you know will bear fruit if you just bear with it, rather a sort of the-group-holding-their-breath kind of silence. And you sense that the group is no longer focused on the task. To help the group relax emotionally and get back to the task, you might need to support the person who is putting himself at stake in "getting an ally"[38]. That is, someone who agrees with what has been said, either on a content, and/or emotional level.

Getting an ally

Carl: *"All this talk about cutting the time for our production process by half bothers me. To be honest, I believe it's both needed and possible, but I actually don't trust you who are leading this change process. You have a lousy track record of following through with change, and the rumor says that both of you are on your way to new jobs…"*

You sense that your 20 some participants are holding their breath. No one utters a word. You put your feet on the ground. You breathe. You wait. Still dead silence. You can see how the person who spoke is starting to pull back physically. He needs help. The group needs help. You decide to intervene.

Facilitator: *"Is there anyone else who shares Carl's concern about staying with the change process? Or, is there anyone else who also doubts the perseverance of X?"*

A few people start to speak, agreeing with parts or all of Carl's statement. You notice how tension decreases and a productive conversation emerges on the importance of securing long-term leadership engagement in the change.

Sometimes there is less of an emergency but still, after taking a few deep breaths, you come to the conclusion that an intervention would support the group to get back to work. The simple act of helping the participants to differentiate is often all that is needed.

Intervening to support task-focus

A group of 25 leaders had gathered to discuss their shared challenges. At this point in the meeting they were working in breakout groups in different rooms. People started to come to me to express dissatisfaction with their working process. They were coming from one group, then from another, then from a third. There were a variety of complaints, everything from poor instructions to irrelevant tasks. I could sense the anxiety that was present and contemplated different ways of proceeding. I consulted the meeting owner and we decided to gather the groups in the large room. I proposed a go-around to support differentiation. Each person briefly shared what was going on for them in relation to the working process. That was all that was needed. They were now eager to go back to work.

Another time a group of about 25 people from neighboring countries gathered to discuss how they could collaborate on various issues of shared concern. A few hours into the meeting, six male voices were dominating the large group conversations and I could see how people were drifting off. I shared my observation and suggested we hear briefly from each one what was on their mind at that moment. The go-around didn't take more than 10-15 minutes. Hearing everyone's voice supported the group to break the stagnating pattern, and the energy for the task that had brought them together returned.

I find that these kinds of breif interventions is time well spent to regain the group's focus and energy.

Principle number six – Any good plan ceases at the point of contact

After stressing planning throughout this book, I want to underline the importance of being flexible in the moment. Before the meeting, we know what we want to achieve, and we know who we need in the room to make that happen. Although in reality we never know what will happen when people come together. We need to stay open to the unfolding process, moment by moment, feeling supported by our plan and yet willing to adjust if reality advises us to do so. If you are the meeting owner as well as the facilitator, you can of course make any changes you would like, though a word of advice is that you inform and sometimes negotiate those changes with the participants. If you are facilitating only, you need to share your observations and ideas for how to proceed with your meeting owner before deciding how to move on.

The example below shows how reality speaks louder than plans when we listen carefully to both content and emotions present in a meeting.

When a plan ceased to be relevant and a magic moment occurred

One of the boundary conditions stated at the start-up of a three-day meeting was that the meeting should be future oriented. There had been enough digging in past events and the meeting-owner feared that the group would lose energy should it continue.

The meeting was off to a tentative start, which made us (meeting owner and facilitator) a bit concerned. We decided to sleep on it and met early in the morning to share our observations and feelings. The meeting owner decided to change his boundary condition "not talking about the past", which he shared with the group as he opened the morning's work. You could see tight shoulders relaxing and sense a deep breath in the group, a pregnant silence. And then a woman spoke: *"I thought I had made peace with the past. Yet being in this room together with you all, talking about the things we've failed to thoroughly address, brings back the pain I have experienced. Three years ago I joined a team with very low self-confidence, and I couldn't understand why. We were all experienced, skilled and engaged in our work. But slowly, the lack of trust and the questioning we experienced from your side (nodding to a few people around the room) also wore me down. Those first two years were very dark years for me; I felt I lost everything I believed was solid in me. We are no longer at that place, but what I realize now is that the pain is still there and is calling for recognition."*

It was clear that she was speaking for the group. Her pain was the group's pain. The respect that was given to this woman as she spoke was a way for everyone to honor their own as well as each other's pain. And the group was ready to move on.

Knowing yourself, and thinking of a meeting you are planning, do any of the principles stand out as particularly relevant for you?

1. *Creating a safe emergency*
2. *Staying out of fixing*
3. *Focusing on the boundaries*
4. *Staying loyal to the task*
5. *Keeping your feet on the ground and breathe*
6. *Remaining flexible as any good plan ceases at the point of contact*

What excites you most about being a facilitator?

What are your biggest concerns about being a facilitator? What can you do to address your concerns, before and during your meeting? How can the principles for facilitation support you?

Imagine…
that you are about to begin your meeting. You have prepared the room to your liking. You greet the participants as they start dropping in, one by one. Your feet are firmly on the ground. If you are not the meeting owner, you feel a mutual trust between you and he/she who owns the meeting/task. Your role is clear. You feel well prepared, ready to meet whatever is to come, believing that whatever happens is what should happen.

If this were your stance, what difference would it make for the success of your meeting…

3.2. Meeting Follow-up and Feedback

It is easy to neglect the follow-up as there can be a significant time delay in strategic development projects. For example, when gathering various stakeholders to define key drivers of change to reach long-term goals, it can take years before those we invited can see the effects of their work. To experience that our contribution matters, we know how important it is to receive feedback. That is why we need to plan for the follow-up before the meeting takes place and not make it into a one-off, such as a thank you e-mail a week after the meeting. A thank you must be followed by regular updates about achievements related to the meeting. Mind you, depending on the scope of the meeting, this feedback process might need to be kept alive for years. So assigning the responsibility for follow-up to someone, or to a function, usually makes sense.

Securing feedback and follow-up

As part of a strategic planning process the whole "pipeline", from product development to manufacturing and sales, was invited to analyze and prioritize the needs for change. Implementation of the decided actions were to begin the following year, beginning with product development, then moving on to manufacturing and logistics. Sales people and customers would start seeing the results in two to three years. This was clearly a diverse group with different needs as far as feedback was concerned. Keeping all participants in the loop was considered key to keeping the energy and speed in the change process. Therefore, people from the business navigation function, who took an active part in planning the meeting as well as being a hub for the strategic planning process, volunteered to keep all the meeting participants informed.

They decided to make a simple newsletter that was sent out every three months to the meeting participants. It included updates on how the work was progressing. It was particularly appreciated by those in sales who often experienced a distance to both product development, production and marketing. This experience gave them a fruitful understanding of the bigger picture, which in turn increased their confidence when meeting the customers.

To give general guidelines for follow-up and feedback is difficult. The examples in this book show a variety of approaches to follow-up. I believe that the best we can do is to step into the shoes of our different participants, see the work from their perspectives and ask ourselves – what, why, when, how and by whom would I like to be informed about what is happening as a consequence of the meeting? And we need to connect that with a bigger picture of the issue of concern, or with the change process.

Another part of the feedback can be to ask the participants how they experienced the meeting process, in case you find it valuable for learning purposes. In many organizations it is something they always do at the close of meetings, or similarly send out feedback forms after major meetings. However, ending a meeting by asking participants to evaluate the meeting process and the facilitation is usually counter-productive. What happens is that you ask the participants to focus on evaluating others when you have spent a whole meeting supporting them in taking responsibility for themselves and the work they produce with others.

So how do we know if we did a good job in planning, designing and facilitating the meeting? The quality of the output gives us a hint;

so does the look on the participants' faces as we close the meeting. Long-term, can we see that the meeting has made a difference? To a large extent, we need to trust our own judgment regarding a meeting's success – or failure.

Think slow

What are the challenges related to the follow-up of the meeting you currently have in mind? And how will you address them?

Who will take responsibility for the long-term follow-up and for giving feedback to those you involve?

Do you have any thoughts or ideas on what kind of feedback and follow-ups that will be relevant for your meeting participants? And what kind of media would be suitable? If you step into the shoes of your different meeting participants – what do you learn about their needs?

If you see the follow-up in a larger perspective – does it affect how you want to handle it?

Imagine…
What difference would it make for the performance, job-satisfaction and change orientation in your workplace if more attention was given to the follow-up phase…

Beyond Meetings – A Culture of Meaningful Involvement

Before leaving the topic of meetings I would like to point out that all the principles, models and tools presented in this book are equally applicable to the meetings we have on a more regular basis. It could be applied to team meetings, supervision meetings, management meetings, project meetings or steering group meetings. Working through the 'steps to meetings with meaning' every once in a while will help to keep your meeting culture alive. Many of the principles in this book may also be used for designing workshops, conferences and other learning activities. The idea of keeping the task front and center is also relevant for team building activities. A clear task or business focus makes the kind of relationships and support structures we need to develop, within and between teams, emerge with greater clarity.

Making a case for a culture of involvement

We are at a paradigm shift when it comes to how we perceive organizing, leadership and our organizations' roles and responsibilities in society. There are many signs that speak loud and clear, for example: urgent and complex challenges that we need to take shared responsibility for, instability and rapid change in our societies and in our markets, the speed of change in technology as well as in people's minds. This inevitably calls for an "upgrade" in how we perceive organizational life. Yet alongside an emerging understanding of the interdependency and insecurity that characterizes the world we live in, we see organizations cling to highly structured methods for strategic planning and business follow-up. We also have more and more refined tools for analyzing competence and reviewing performance on individual level. And the pyramid is still the way we illustrate our organizations, although sometimes with the addition of vertical lines to describe our business processes. Were we to capture how people actually need to communicate, collaborate and make decisions, the picture would be very different. Consequently, the needs for leadership, structure and support would emerge as very different from what we have in place today.

The principles and approaches presented in this book are steps to support this shift in mindset. They challenge the hierarchical model, but only if you want them to. You can apply the principles within the current framework of hierarchy and step by step move higher in the levels of involvement as well as critically question the "non-negotiables" thus widening the room to maneuver. Collecting experiences of what a group of diverse people are capable of accomplishing helps us develop the courage and wisdom to take yet another step towards a culture of involvement.

However, many organizations still rely heavily on hierarchy and management by control. If you are a middle manager or a change agent in one of those organizations and want to challenge your corporate culture, you probably need to navigate with caution. You may invite your team to a meaning-making process to begin with, where the risk is fairly small. You might just be questioned regarding the time you allocate for the activity, the design you choose and your facilitation style might raise some eyebrows. The effects usually become quickly apparent; such as the smooth implementation of a business plan that has been well understood due to your involvement process. Coaching is another low-risk method for involvement. The levels of involvement and engagement presented in Part One of this book are equally applicable when coaching individuals as well as teams.

Meaningful involvement processes also help bridge the "strategy-operations gap", which many organizations struggle with. Senior managers often have difficulty communicating meaningfully with co-workers and middle managers and vice versa. This is understandable since they often live and work in different realities. When we involve all hierarchical levels in development work, senior managers increase their understanding of the day-to-day reality, which makes them better decision-makers. Simultaneously, co-workers and managers involved in daily operations develop their understanding of the bigger picture and the long-term perspective which enables them to have a more proactive and developmental approach to their tasks.

To be able to navigate in today's world we need to make peace with uncertainty and we must learn to thrive in ambiguity. We must come to terms with our need for heroic leaders; leaders who know and can give us the answers; leaders who can take care of our fears and our insecurities for us. We must dare to trust leaders who have the courage to put their trust in us, leaders who invite us into rooms where there are no answers. Meaningful involvement supports us in building our collective capacity to do that. It is much more exciting and safer to be in the unknown together with others – and it is more fulfilling to make decisions together with others who also care.

"...human beings have a fundamental need to strive together in collective action... Our hope lies in our capacity to depend on each other and share responsibility for sustaining ourselves, our families, our environments, and our futures."

The Relational Center[39]

Let us create organizations that are capable of making a difference in our world and are worthy of our engagement, because we are worth it and the world needs it[40]. Cultures of meaningful involvement safeguard us from isolation, they foster our humanity and wisdom, and they enable us to develop our courage and our sense of responsibility – for our tasks, for each other and for our environment. As human beings we want to be of use, but we don't want to be used. We want to support one another and we want to feel supported. We want those who ask us questions to listen to our answers with a willingness to be changed.

We are ready to take shared responsibility for our future.

How would you describe the culture at your workplace as it connects to involvement?

What risks, if any, can you foresee if you were to initiate more meaningful involvement processes? For yourself, and for the people you lead and/or involve, for your organization?

Which levels of involvement would you regard as safe? Challenging? Too high risk?

Imagine…
If more organizational cultures could be described as cultures for meaningful involvement, how would that impact on our society…

Words of Gratitude

I wouldn't have much experience to share without Eugenio Moliní, Sandra Janoff and Marvin Weisboard. As my role models and teachers, you help me connect with and be guided by my passion for meaningful involvement.

Rick Maurer's sharp thinking around change and his approach to teaching greatly supports me to meaningfully connect my work with leading change.

My managers through my years of employment, you gave me the space and trust to experiment. Gisela Wasmouth, Bo Göransson, Britt Hagström and Christina Nilensjö – thank you.

I feel very grateful to all my clients, and the challenging assignments you give me. I learn from you every day and every minute.

I am also grateful for the times I have designed and facilitated meetings that haven't been successful. Working with this book has turned painful experiences into nourishment and a little bit of wisdom.

I want to thank you who ask me questions about my work. Your questions force me to "think slow" and to formulate myself, making my tacit knowledge more explicit and possible to share with others. A special thanks to Hans-Åke Persson who, probably unwittingly, ignited my writing process by asking: *"What is the thought-process behind what you do?"*

Friends, your thorough, critical and supportive reading and subsequent feedback means the world to me. Yannis Angelis, Ursula Erasmus, Angela Johansson, Kinna Persson, Eva Wendt, Eugenio Moliní, Oliver Kozak, Shanil Haricharan - thank you.

Mette Sandahl Bengtsson, you gave me a great idea for the book – thank you.

Kevin Foster and Stephen Parsons, your generous help at a critical moment is much appreciated.

Göran, my personal editor, critic and life partner. My appreciation of your involvement in this book-project – with your sharp mind, esthetic eyes and warm heart – is difficult to put into words.

Thank you to our daughters who, during my writing process, kept asking me: *"Mom, how many pages have you written now? Wow, that many!"* For the record girls, it is 163.

Books That Can Inspire

Hopefully, reading this book has made you hungry for more. If so, here is a list of books that have inspired me in my work with meetings with meaning, and in supporting organizations in developing a culture of involvement.

About planning, designing and facilitating meetings

Doyle, Michael et al., *Facilitator's Guide to Participatory Decision-making (2007)*

A hands-on book about meeting design and facilitation. It describes a number of techniques and the authors are very explicit in how to use them. They advocate a more intervening facilitating style than the one described in this book, which can support you further in finding your own style.

Holman, Peggy, *The Change Handbook (3 volume set): The Definitive Resource on Today's Best Methods for Engaging Whole Systems (2007)*

The title says it all. If you want to know more about all the great methods that are out there, here is where to look. It keeps coming in new editions. The one I got has got a font that is so large that it makes it hard to read.

Moliní, Eugenio, *Libro sobre participación genuina (2012)* Accessible as an e-book at www.molini.es

This beautiful book about genuine participation processes is at the moment of writing accessible only to those who read Spanish. If you are ready to make the most of involvement, inviting people to co-create, this is your source of inspiration. Moliní makes a clear case of what kind of values and commitment it takes and what you can gain when you have the courage to do it. His honest and generous sharing of his own successes as well as failures instills hope that we can do it.

Van Haastrecht, Rob and Scheepbouwer, Martin, *Thinking Backwards – the Art of Problem Solving in Business (2011)*
This little book is a healthy questioning of much of what we think we know about problem solving in business.

Weisboard, Marvin and Janoff, Sandra, *Don't Just Do Something, Stand There! Ten Principles for Leading Meetings That Matter (2007)*
When we are in the facilitator's role we need to feel supported. No other book, and no other role models have made me feel as supported. A must-read for facilitators.

Weisboard, Marvin and Janoff, Sandra, *The Future Search Handbook (2012)*
This is your guide to planning and conducting a Future Search Conference. It is a wonderful method for finding common ground and mobilizing for action when stakes are high and diverse groups of people need to come together and do something.

About change

Keegan, Robert and Lahey, Lisa Laskow, *Immunity to Change, How to Overcome It and Unlock the Potential in Yourself and Your Organization, (2001)*
This group of Harvard professors has a beautiful way of honoring our resistance to change, both on an individual and on a group level. Describing resistance as an immune system invites us to meet our own, and other people's resistance with love and care.

Maurer, Rick, *Beyond the Wall of Resistance. Why 70% of All Changes Still Fail – and What You Can Do About It, (2010)*

Maurer, Rick, *Why Don't You Want What I Want? How to Win Support for Your Ideas without Hard Sell, Manipulation or Power Plays (2002)*
What can I say, I have learned so much from Rick Maurer. I share his models and thinking around change in this book. His language is straight-forward and accessible. I also want to recommend his website www.rickmaurer.com where he generously shares his thinking around change through great models, tools, podcasts and videos. His work is firmly grounded in Gestalt theory and practice without confusing the reader with Gestalt jargon.

About leadership and teams
Arenvi, Katharina, Bramsen, Annika, Giege, Ulf, *Ta ledarskapet till nästa nivå (2011)*
A very accessible book (for Swedish speakers that is) on what leadership development is really about. They base their work on the latest research about adult development. Certain developmental phases in leadership would be more conducive for creating a culture of involvement.

Sewerin, Thomas, *En plats i stolen – En arbetsbok för grupper om grupper (1996)*
This is a jewel that I keep coming back to. Only in Swedish though. Some beautiful ideas on how to support teams to "think slow".

Wheelan, Susan A. *Creating Effective Teams (2013)*
Wheelan has done extensive research on what high performing teams really do. One encouraging finding is that they spend 70-80% of the their time talking about goals and tasks, and the next most frequent statements made are of a supportive character.

About learning organizations and other related topics
Hofstede, et al., *Cultures and Organizations: Software of the Mind, third edition: Intercultural Cooperation and Its Importance For Survival (2010)* This is a great orientation in intercultural cooperation.

Isaacs, William, *Dialogue and the Art of Thinking Together: A Pioneering Approach to Communicating in Business and in Life (1996)*
This is a book that I believe will never be out-dated. Full of inspiring case-studies, and he really transmits a belief in the power of true dialogue.

Johnson, Barry, *Polarity Management, Identifying and Managing Unsolvable Problems (1996)*
Barry Johnson takes the creative idea of acknowledging the complexity of polarities in organizational development all the way. It really makes you think.

Kahneman, Daniel, *Thinking Fast and Slow (2011)*
Kahneman has raised a much needed warning flag for just trusting our intuition, what he calls system 1 thinking. I have borrowed the term "thinking slow" from his vocabulary, which refers to what he calls system 2 thinking.

Senge, Peter M, *The Fifth Discipline: The Art and Practice of The Learning Organization: Second edition (2006)*
Senge was the pioneer of learning organizations with his first edition in 1993. It's a book that remains relevant.

Senge, Peter M, Jaworski, Joseph, Flowers, Betty Sue, Scharmer, C Otto, Presence: *Exploring Profound Change in People, Organizations and Society (2005)*
As readers, we are invited to join in an explorative conversation which includes everything that makes up a rich conversation; uncertainty, personal stories, disagreements, shared insights, anxiety, joy, confusion…

Zeldin, Theodor, *Conversation – How Talk Can Change Our Lives (1998)*
This book gives hope. Simple conversations can change our lives for the better. High quality conversations are simple, but not easy.

About Gestalt theory and methodology

Mackewn, Jennifer, *Developing Gestalt Counselling (1997)*
This is a book about counseling and psychotherapy, not about Gestalt in organizations. But for the reader who would like an introduction to Gestalt, its roots and main theoretical concepts, that's what you'll get. And Mackewn really captures the artistry of the Gestalt approach.

Nevis, Ed, *Organizational Consulting – A Gestalt Approach (1987)*
Ed Nevis was one of the pioneers in bringing Gestalt theory into the organizational world. This book is not a very easy read, in my opinion, but for the interested reader the effort invested pays off.

Appendix 1.

Template for planning & designing a Meeting with Meaning

Meeting headline:

Date and time:

Location:

Meeting participants:

Others who need to participate and their role
– As task-owner, facilitator, presenters, experts, documenter, etc:

Relevant background/situation right now:

Goals

Results (to be achieved by the end of the meeting/workshop)**:**

Effects (more long-term desired effects)**:**

Relevant boundaries:

Brief agenda:

To bring/prepare:

Design:

Time	**Content & Design** *Keep the phases in mind: warming up, doing the work, closing*	**Responsible person**	**Purpose**	**Comments**

Appendix 2.

I want to involve people BUT...
...what if there is too much resistance...
...what if I lose control...
...I wish there was more room to influence...
...what if they don't care...

WHAT KIND OF MEETING ARE YOU PLANNING?

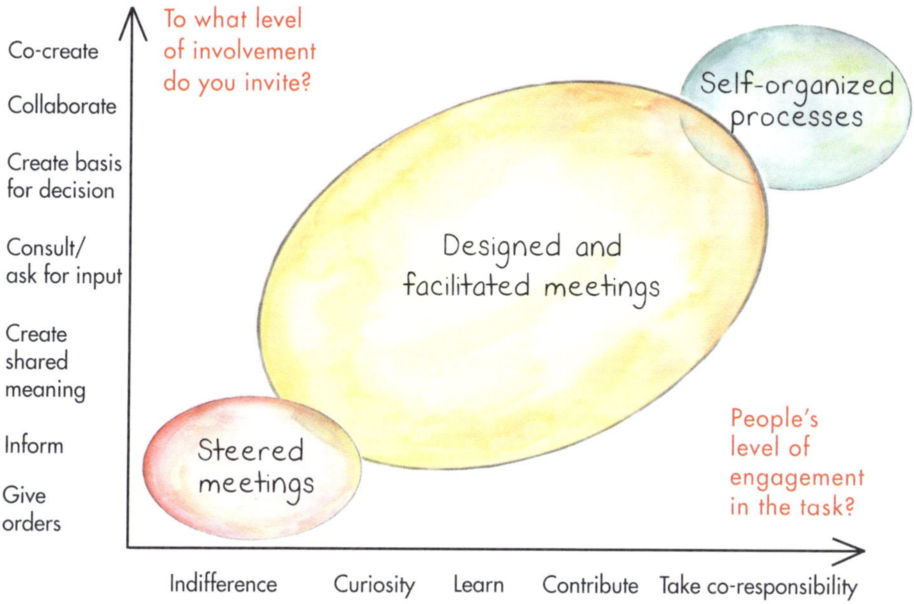

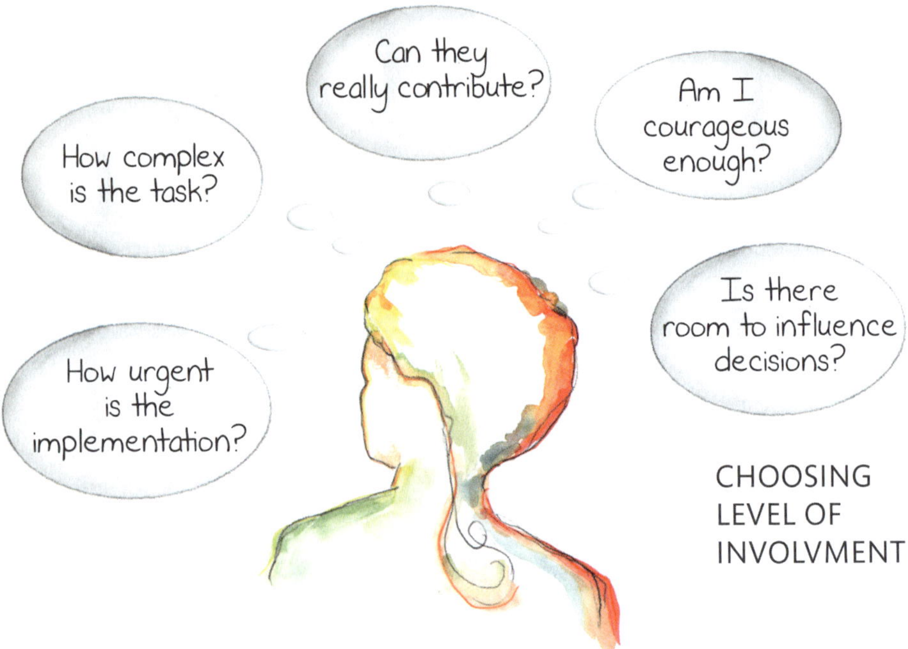

CHOOSING
LEVEL OF
INVOLVMENT

BASED ON THE WORK OF RICK MAURER

THREE SOURCES OF RESISTANCE

BASED ON THE WORK OF RICK MAURER

6. Meeting Follow-up
5. Facilitating the meeting
4. Ensuring healthy working conditions
3. Designing the meeting
2. Planning the meeting - who to involve and invite
1. Creating the Foundation - goals and boundaries

PHASES IN A MEETING
Warming up
To the task
To people
Doing the work
Exploring and differentiating
Integrating and finding common ground
Concluding and deciding
Closing
The Task
The Process

IN A MEETING PARTICIPANTS MIND...
25% After
25% Now
25% Before
25% Outer Space
HOW CAN WE SUPPORT PRESENCE?

WHAT IF...

...they get bored...
...a few dominate...
...there is a conflict...
...they all turn against me...
...they come up with bad ideas...

SIX PRINCIPLES FOR FACILITATING

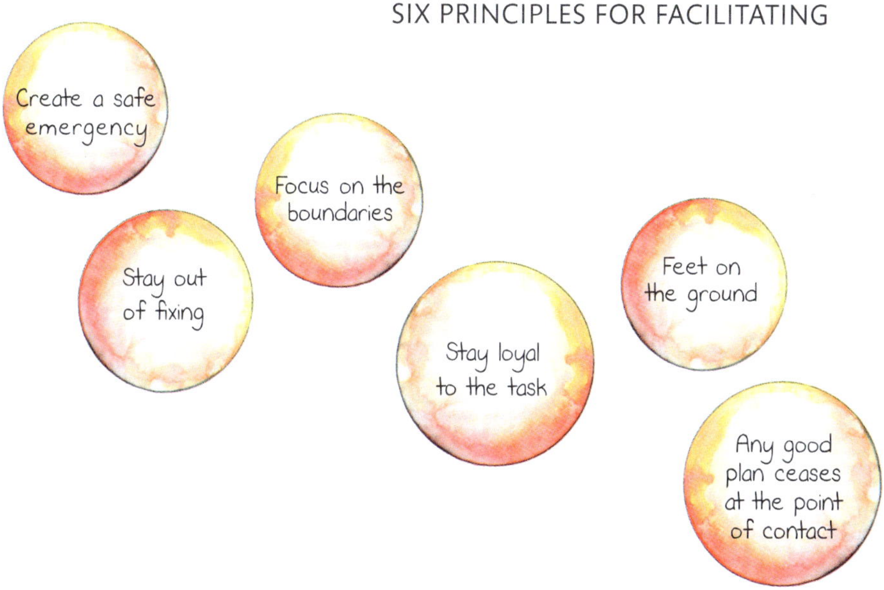

Appendix 3.

Endnotes

[1] The Gestalt Roots Conference V, Bommersvik, Sweden 2012.

[2] Jack Martin Leith told me that he found his inspiration to this quote in an article by Gary Hamel (Fortune. New York: June 23, 1997).

[3] Open Space Technology is a method suitable for inviting highly engaged people to a high level of involvement. See www.openspaceworld.org.

[4] The terms used on the vertical axes of the model are inspired by Bryan Smith's description of different kinds of leadership; Telling, Selling, Testing, Consulting, Co-creating, in The Fifth Discipline Fieldbook: Strategies for Building a Learning Organization (1994 Nicholas Brealey, p 314). The horizontal line, as well as the idea of combining the vertical with the horizontal, is inspired by Eugenio Moliní, www.molini.es.

[5] A quote from an interview with Tom Stratton, a formal student at The Gestalt Institute of Cleveland, an institute that offers training with a Gestalt approach, www.gestaltcleveland.org.

[6] For more information on Rick Maurer and his thinking on change, visit his website www.maurer.com, or see his books on change presented in Books That Can Inspire. The Cycle of Change is based on the Institute of Cleveland's Gestalt Cycle of Experience. I am using a version of the cycle, inspired by Ursula Erasmus, a fellow student at the Influence, Action, Change program at the Gestalt Institute of Cleveland.

[7] Among other studies, see "Making Change Work" (IBM New York, 2008) Hans Henrik Jorgensen, Lawrence Owen, and Andreas Neus, and "The Inconvenient Truth About Change Management, Why it isn't working and what to do about it." (McKinsey, 2008) Scott Keller and Carolyn Aiken.

[8] Brain research shows that the part of the brain called amygdala gets activated when we feel threatened. When that happens we don't register properly what is going on around us, as our whole being is focused on survival. Daniel Goleman calls it "amygdala hijack" in his book Emotional Intelligence (1996).

[9] The administrative bodies of the Bahá'í Faith at all levels use a distinctive method of non-adversarial decision-making called Consultation.

[10] Didas Tumuhairwe is the HR manager at The Supreme Audit Institution in Uganda. Didas shared his thoughts on change at the Human Resource Management workshop run by AFROSAI-E in Pretoria, South Africa, October 2013.

[11] This is an example of what in Gestalt theory is called the Paradoxical Theory of Change. By allowing *what is* to get under your skin, change starts to happen. See article by Arnold Beisser: www.gestalt.org/arnie.htm.

[12] Using Gestalt terminology, this can be described as leaders being confluent with their teams. For a deeper understanding of confluence and other so called "styles of contact", see Books That Can Inspire.

[13] From their book "Don't Just Do Something – Stand There!", see Books That Can Inspire.

[14] Another way to describe this is by using the Gestalt term polarities, that is two opposites that are interrelated. For more on polarities, Polarity Management by Barry Johnson is a good read, see Books That Can Inspire.

[15] The idea of dividing goals into results and effects comes from Eugenio Moliní. I'm not sure he still does, but I do.

[16] My colleague and friend Janne Nilsson coined the term "Relational Capacity" and I've taken a strong liking to it. Depending on the complexity of that tasks we are handling together, we may need more or less relational capacity. Using the word capacity helps us see that strong enough relationships is something we can actively build.

[17] For more information on what a "whole system approach" can be, check out, Don't Just Do Something… by Janoff and Weisboard, see Books That Can Inspire.

[18] Moliní makes a strong and clear case for clarity on why people need to participate in their own right in his book Participación Genuína, see Books That Can Inspire.

[19] There are a number of group development theories that all describe the same pattern. I recommend Susan Wheelan's book on teams, see Books That Can Inspire.

[20] Source: Holone newsletter nb 1, February 2013. www.holone.se

[21] Inspired by Claus Janssen's The Four Rooms of Change (1995) where one room is confusion. The four rooms are contentment, denial, confusion and inspiration.

[22] To learn more about Samuel West's findings on creativity and happiness at work, see www.samuelwest.se.

[23] A matrix is an organizational structure that facilitates the horizontal flow of skills, information and cross-border collaboration.

[24] I learned from Adam Kincel, a Gestalt Practitioner and large group researcher, that in groups with more than 30-40 people family dynamics are no longer at play, but rather social and political dynamics. This fits well with my experience.

[25] Some 25 years ago, Seàn Gaffney, a Gestalt Practitioner and teacher, drew the picture of what is in a participant's head at the beginning of a meeting or a training workshop. It has been with me ever since.

[26] I picked up this idea of how to start a challenging meeting in a way that supports participants' responsibility from Eugenio Moliní. I have since made good use of it in many meetings.

[27] This is inspired by Rick Maurer where he in his book, Why Don't You Want What I Want, discusses what it takes to explore effectively (Chapter 8, p 126), see Books That Can Inspire.

[28] SWOT is a structured method for analyzing Strengths, Weaknesses, Opportunities and Threats related to any project or business issue.

[29] I learned this from Eugenio Moliní and I have found this a simple act of clarifying that whatever is going on in a group of people that are interdependent is the group's responsibility. It seems to support groups to see the group's common concern more clearly, which in turns supports constructive collaboration.

[30] From Don't Just Do Something – Stand There (2007, p 82), by Janoff and Weisboard, see Books That Can Inspire.

[31] Using a so-called "talking stick" means that he/she who holds the stick has the word. I have found that it, when used at the right moment, supports us in speaking our truth as well as our curiosity in, and respect for one another.

[32] For the reader who is familiar with Gestalt Theory, the three phases in a meeting connect to the Cycle of Experience. It's about creating a design that supports the

group in mobilizing energy for about the same thing – the task – at about the same time and act, i.e. do the needed work, and then close – digest the experience and come to a place of satisfaction and rest. To know more about the cycle of experience see Books That Can Inspire.

[33] This sentence is inspired by Theodor Zeldin's beautiful little book, Conversation – How Talk Can Change Our Lives (1998: p 3).

[34] This quiz is from Marvin Weisboard's and Sandra Janoff's book, Don't Just Do Something, Stand There! (2007: p 31)

[35] I have borrowed the term "safe emergency" from the Gestalt Institute of Cleveland where it is used to describe brief experiments designed for learning purposes. By using the expression in a meeting context, I believe I may have slightly altered its meaning.

[36] The self-organizing roles are from Janoff and Weisboard: Don't Just Do Something – Stand There" (2007: p 75), see Books That Can Inspire.

[37] This is inspired from Janoff's and Weisboard's book Don't Just Do Something – Stand There. The title itself is a paraphrase of the fact that "nature hates vacuum – so the more you do, the less the participants do".

[38] See Don't Just Do Something – Stand There (2007: p 104-115) by M Weisboard and S Janoff. Helping a person to get an ally, asking the "anyone else question", is a direct learning from Janoff and Weisboard, but of course this is my interpretation of what they are saying in their book. I advise you to go to the source where you will find much more on when and how to intervene when facilitating meetings. For workshops on facilitation skills, do contact s.janoff@futuresearch.net.

[39] This is the Relational Center's mission statement:
"We assume that human beings have a fundamental need to strive together in collective action. In fact, the more we try to overcome complex problems by ourselves, the more we suffer. Our hope lies in our capacity to depend on each other and share responsibility for sustaining ourselves, our families, our environments, and our futures." For more information about the Relational Center and their great work, visit www.relationalcenter.org

[40] This quote is inspired by Gestalt Practitioner Ulf Zwedberg, who has said "let's create organizations that are worthy of our engagement". Thank you for putting it so well.